MY BREATH
IN ART:
ACTING FROM
WITHIN

BEATRICE MANLEY

AN APPLAUSE ORIGINAL

My Breath in Art: Acting From Within
Beatrice Manley
Copyright © 1998 by Beatrice Manley

Library of Congress Cataloging-in-Publication Data

Manley, Beatrice.
    My breath in art : acting from within / by Beatrice Manley.
       p. cm.
    ISBN 1-55783-281-1 (pbk.)
    1. Acting--Breathing exercises.   I. Title.
PN2071.B74M36   1997
792'.028--dc21   97-19329
                                          CIP

British Library Cataloging-in-Publication Data

A catalogue record of this book is available from the British Library

APPLAUSE BOOKS

211 West 71st Street
New York, NY 10023
Phone (212) 496-7511
Fax: (212) 721-2856

CONTENTS

To the memory of my father, his talent and discipline

INTRODUCTION

He got no science
He got no speed
He don't change his tactics
and I just picked him off.

—Muhammad Ali

The most important thing about acting is honesty. If you can fake that, you've got it made.

— George Burns

The fascinating thing about acting is its seeming contradiction. On the one hand, a shadow of a thought, a fragment of memory, can ignite emotion. On the other, in that intimate, fragile moment, we must speak in a real voice with a degree of projection.

1.

Young performers believe that acting is charisma and technique is something they learn in school and discard as soon as they can get rid of the teacher.

Why do we teach breathing, speech, and the use of the body? It is because the liveliness of the imagination is dulled and the release of emotions is blocked when the voice and body are dysfunctional.

Acting with technique leads to an act of faith — we trust that the body will respond without our making sure that it does. It means knowing that after breathing out, the breath will return to the body by itself. If we keep our faith, we will trust the breath to do the acting for us. The imagination connected to the breath engages us in larger and ever larger concepts; concepts without which we could not have been inspired to imagine. We cannot have ecstasy without breath.

There is a technique for everything; for speaking, moving, breathing, for courage, for charisma — that certain something. But charisma is in the breath and the muscles and we can't have that "something" when we hold the breath and tense the muscles.

In the beginning we are separate from technique. It belongs to someone else—our teacher or our teacher's teacher. We feel it is being grafted onto us. One day we discover that technique has become a natural response, embedded in the flesh, second nature, and then our technique is who we are.

OUR INHERITANCE

The twelfth Witch bestowed Talent on the newborn, the Beloved. But the thirteenth Witch cackled that Talent wouldn't be fulfilled until the child learned Technique. Given the resistance that performers bring to technique, it is no wonder the thirteenth Witch cackled. Even back then it was difficult to convince us that Technique would not spoil Talent.

Sometimes Talent manages to transcend a lack of Technique. Somehow we reveal what we feel. But it is a struggle, and Talent can't protect us. We damage the voice. We stress the muscles. We don't come out and say so, but we feel uncomfortable and conclude that acting is hard. When we act without breath, acting *is* hard. When we act on the breath we connect up with what we deeply know, have always known.

All the acting technique that we've learned in the last sixty or more years, starting, of course, with Stanislavsky, are enormously important, but the breath comes first; the ebb and flow of a moving breath carries emotions and ideas through the body.

My breath gathers information, acquires knowledge, from the outside world and brings it into my life system. Passing over the inner organs, the breath pulls my life experience up through the torso to the words and gestures. It fills the words with emotion and meaning. I hear with my breath, I get frightened with my breath, I fall in love and the breath knows it first, I feel furious and the breath feels it first.

2.

It takes time to incorporate a new technique into our lives. The mind rejects it. Why be uncomfortable, why suffer? But it gets in little by little. The Chinese water method, drop by drop by drop, is torture only in Fu Manchu movies. In learning, it has its bright side; the more slowly a technique is learned, the more deeply it is understood and retained.

If there is a little crack in the infrastructure, there will be a trace of that weakness in every aspect of our work. Going back to learn a new technique is hard on the ego. Before we master it, there is a gap and we lose identity. It's a combination of ego and fear. One big combination.

3.

If only we could be apprentices hanging out around some great genius, night and day, and learn acting by breathing it in. I wouldn't mind hauling ashes from the fireplace and scrubbing floors like some waif out of a Dickens novel if in the end I'd be able to act the way I know in my heart I can.

But we are stuck with acting lessons. And acting technique books. It's risky for a performer to read about acting techniques. Reading Stanislavsky when I was young was no picnic. I read the book much too literally and was sure I was the most insincere actress in the whole world. It wasn't Stanislavsky's fault. He loved performers.

Performers take in information in many ways — the least of which may be through the written word. Yet ideas must be disseminated. So, I'm going to write a nice book about acting that even I wouldn't be scared to read.

1

THE BREATH

The force that through
the green fuse drives the flower

—Dylan Thomas

We can't take our eyes off the amaryllis when it is in bloom, when it is performing. But its performance didn't start at the top. It started from below, a little green stem growing out of a rough bulb in a pot of earth. Little by little its talent, inherent in the roots, unfolds into the flower.

We can't get to our Talent without the Breath and the Words.

1.

Whenever our acting takes an unpredictable, magical turn, it is because, somehow, the breath has touched our intuition and come up with what had been hidden in our thoughts and emotions.

The breath is both unconscious and conscious, involuntary and voluntary. The breath works in secret; even if we don't breathe it breathes. And as if that weren't enough of a gift, we are able, at will, to breathe more or to breathe less. But until it's brought to our attention, we don't bother much about it. And as long as enough air comes into the body to sustain life, well . . . we make do. But to be an athlete, a pianist, a singer, a performer, a little breath is not enough.

Making-Believe when we're kids is basically no different from making-believe we're Queen Gertrude or Hamlet. But growing up we get a little uptight, compress our breath and lose the joy of playing the game.

It starts early in life. In the sandbox.

We are playing happily. Suddenly the other baby whacks us. Startled, we hold our breath, then we bawl. Crying brings a comforting parent to our side. *It also releases the breath.*

Off we go to elementary school.

Some kid hauls off and whacks us. The body remembers to hold the breath. Then we cry. But we are too old to be

held and comforted. The kids make fun of us. We stop crying but continue to hold our breath.

We are in high school. We have learned not to cry. We
now have other ways of dealing with stress — hold the
breath and tense the shoulders. Our body has established its
patterns. By the time we get to drama school we're a mess.

When the breath stops moving, the tension created in
the body blocks the flow of emotions and ideas. The potential of passion is felt but none of its power. We have to be
taught techniques for releasing those tensions.

Acting has a different feel when there is no breath.
There is a pressure inside the body. This pressure is reas-
suring because it feels like hard work and hard work will be
rewarded by a good performance, will it not? There is an
emotional investment in trying hard. When we act on the
breath we feel a lightness we don't trust.

2.

Think of breath as a feeling in the body, like swimming.
When we were kids we would stay in the water so long we
could feel, at night in bed, that we were still swimming; a
feeling hard to describe in words but one that we deeply and
confidently understood.

Of necessity, the teacher has to use words to explain a
technique, but the performer has to change these words into
body language, body knowledge. We respond to a feeling
without repeating the words that were used to teach us
about that feeling. The inner dialogue which explains the
explanation is a wearying habit and very hard to break.

I do not think in words.
— Albert Einstein

PHYSICALLY FEELING A THEORY

Baby is two years old. The Parent/Teacher starts to inundate Baby with the Theory and Technique of Potty Training. Baby couldn't care less. But one day something happens. Baby recognizes a Physical Feeling and puts it together with all that Theory and goes and sits on the Potty. The first great step in civilization has been taken. That night Parents call Grandma long distance and Baby gets a lollipop. From then on, Baby trusts that Feeling. It need never be explained in words. Baby knows what it is.

When we turn theory over to the body, eventually talent and the body's mysterious knowledge figure it out. A skill, no matter how long it takes to acquire through conscious effort, is truly learned only when it is internalized.

3.

A graduate student asked one day in an oral reading class: "*Why* do we need breath when we read?" It wasn't a question so much as exasperation, an eagerness to get to the good stuff, the story part. Since we don't believe without hard proof, I asked her to get rid of her breath, take vocal aim at the wall and count, loudly, to twenty-eight. That was proof.

- Try counting without breath to see how it feels.
- Next, count, and just before it becomes impossible to go on, breathe and continue.
- On the last try, breathe a little sooner, without waiting for the discomfort to set in, and keep counting.

Accepting that breath is necessary is the first step. An actress, slowing down the exercise, said: "I was exploring the places the breath was taking me." That is too self-conscious.

Follow the breath the way we follow a puppy out for its walk. It is unpremeditated, unself-conscious exploration. The puppy is impelled by its senses, not its mind.

Getting by on the least amount of air has become habitual. For a quick experience of breathing:

Run up some hills to lose control of the breathing. Gasping for air, walk a bit, then lie down and observe how the breath moves. Breaths are irregular. They are short, long, deep, shallow. They are whatever they are. Don't control them to make them correct. No two snowflakes are alike; no two breaths are alike. Finally, notice how breathing regulates itself and becomes calm, rhythmic, ongoing.

Casually watch your breathing as it restores itself to normal. Recognize what the breath does when it is neither compressed nor interfered with. It's the way a baby breathes when it's comfortably asleep.

Once the breath has quieted down, don't take control of it again. As if blind, learn to follow the breath's movement instead of having the breath follow the dictates of the conscious mind. It takes practice.

4.

We never know when the mind will grasp a concept and the body will master its technique.

On the ceiling of the Sistine Chapel, God's and Adam's fingers reach toward each other and they never touch. In our learning, there is that moment when the fingers touch; when Concept and Technique meet.

≈≈≈

So far, this is breathing that is fundamental and biological. Now let's apply the breath to performing.

THE BREATH IN ACTING

Breathing naturally, we let that breath receive our thoughts. This is an organic, natural response, requiring nothing from us. Breath and thoughts will be folded into words and gestures.

It was during my rehearsals of the Molly Bloom soliloquy from James Joyce's *Ulysses* that I glimpsed what it was like to act with the breath. At first, I was careful of pacing and energy. But at some point I happened to work in real time, letting the thoughts come when they would. When breath brought the ideas up into my mind there was something deeply logical about the timing of my laughter and tears. When I lost the trust and jumped ahead of the breath in my response, I couldn't keep from controlling the material and subtly manipulating it.

When I follow my breath, I don't have to reach out for the emotional peaks. The emotions flow to a peak with my breath as it crests inside my body. I can't tell the breath from the acting.

Different people breathe differently. The guy who sells newspapers in New York around Times Square breathes differently than does the garage mechanic in Burbank.

5.

Breath is always emotional. With the slightest ripple of change, the breath changes. We experience fear, laughter, anxiety first in the breath. When we perform, it's as if our breath hears the cue even before our ears do, as if our breath sees before we see. Images and memories float onto the breath without prompting from the rational mind. The breath touches intuition, that part of ourselves where our native talent is sheltered. If we know how to breathe, *in-*

tending our thought to mesh with the breath is enough. It will.

The audience breathes in the images we carry on our breath. If we don't breathe the character into the body, neither we nor the audience will find the character convincing.

MISTAKES HAPPEN

We may, before the breath completes its cycle, either jump ahead of it to the word or think too much about it and slow it down. If we are too eager, we jump ahead to "act" before we feel that faint inner impulse connecting breath to the action. For example: an actress was flirting in a scene before she felt the emotion on the inside of her body. She was using only her eye muscles for twinkling and her dimples for smiling. She could almost get away with it, but not quite. We can make like we feel it instead of feeling it. That impulse to flirt starts in the body on the breath. Only after that, almost simultaneously, is it revealed through the eyes. Think of having two bodies. The inner body has the emotions first and the outer body reveals them. Blood flows to the cheek and we blush.

≈≈≈

We can become too careful about taking breaths — like having a full tank of gas and topping it with a bit more.

When the breath moves through the body without resistance, the lightest thought is revealed effortlessly.

Breath is Power without coercion. Acting on the breath, we need not force ourselves to produce emotion.

Don't bypass the breath and jump to the words.

A deeply satisfying breath gives physical comfort. Physical comfort induces mental pleasure. Mental pleasure is confidence. We can work at being confident for years through psychological persuasion. We can get it faster through the breath.

Spontaneity is found first in the breath.

Following the breath is following subtle rhythm.

Breath enhances the word the way odors enhance memory.

When we feel the breath at the word; then we speak.

When we feel the breath at the gesture; then we gesture. Gesturing without breath, the breath gets pressed down in the body, stuck somewhere in the torso, while the hand is somewhere out in space. That's disconnection.

≈≈≈

We don't always need to use the largest breath. Addressing the Emperor from across the courtyard, we need a larger breath than when we are talking to a friend who is right beside us. A smaller breath doesn't mean a shallow breath.

An actor who plays golf explained his version: Holding the club, the golfer always swings full and large. There are times when only the shorter part of the full swing is needed.

The breath always flows in and out of the lungs, but sometimes we use only the part of the breath that is nearest the word.

Who knows what comes first—the breath or the idea? Let's not take everything too literally. Breathe because it feels good. It's in our biological contract. And the rest happens.

6.

Breath is an ongoing movement in the body. The performer follows the breath as a cue to speak just as a surfer waits for the wave. The whole person of the surfer is ready;

the mind, the training, cellular intelligence, the body's alertness — there is no separation. There is just the superb familiarity with the wave and the willingness to go with it.

The breath — elusive, powerful, sensual, spiritual — is the cosmic glue bonding mind and body. Thoughts flow to words on the breath.

THE PATH OF THE BREATH

If we know how to breathe, we are centered. When air comes into the body, it comes in, at first, all over; it's like a paisley design. Then it forms into a column of air as it moves through the mouth and out of the body. That column of air is a Path.

To be centered is to have gathered our strength together. The mind, the whole body, the breath, the tongue are joined in expressing what we feel. It is what all these techniques are about: closing the gap between ourselves and IT, getting as close to the character as possible, without the least chink of space between performer and character.

TO FEEL THE PATH

We need to feel the landscape inside the mouth, to know the terrain as though we have studied a map, to feel the location of vowels and consonants and to sense, instantly, when they are out of bounds. To feel the Path is to feel an EE vowel across the blade of the tongue, and a D consonant touching the back of the upper teeth, and an R popping off in the middle of the tongue instead of at the sides.

We need to have awareness of the rest of the body's terrain as well; we want to feel when shoulders are not lined up with hip bones, when the chin is pushing forward too far ahead of the chest. We want to feel the difference between being in profile and facing front, and to be aware of a mindless gesture we may have made.

The Path gives structure to a performance. It gives coherence to ideas and emotions.

It is from ordinary physical techniques that we first get the feeling of the Path. Imagination takes it from there, and we begin to feel the scenario of our script roll out like a red carpet. And we are one with it.

May the Breath be with you.

2

THE WAY OF WORDS

1.

The young actor was exciting. Any expression that was intensely emotional he could access quickly and with passion. What more can we ask of a performer? But between improvisations he was miserably uncomfortable; he couldn't sit without squirming, his neck was stiff, his voice rasped. He was like a promising but undisciplined tennis player hitting the balls all over the court; he had no idea where in his mouth his words were coming from or landing.

I wanted to teach him how to use his breath to free his body from tension. I wanted to teach him the power of words and how to avail himself of their complexity. His acting depended on his emotional response to character. He had plenty of that and it served him well. However, he had nothing but force with which to act. He didn't care about vowels and consonants. What can the movement of the tongue possibly have to do with emotion and insight into personality? What has the K consonant got to do with Hamlet? He didn't need acting lessons. He needed to harness a raw, chaotic force into a talent of subtlety, of nuance, to go along with his great emotional involvement.

A piano teacher explains that the dynamics of sound — soft, dramatic, yearning — are produced not only by an emotional response to the music but very largely by the way the hands and which part of the hands move over the keyboard. "Every finger has three knuckles and each knuckle moves the finger for a different quality of sound..."

If a pianist believes that the use of a particular knuckle is partially responsible for the emotional quality of the music, why can't an actor accept that the dynamic of sound comes not only from an emotional response to the material but also from where on the tongue vowels and consonants take place?

This is the infrastructure of performance.

2.

The Performer: "Doesn't the word start in the gut?"

The Teacher: "No. Words belong to the body but not to the gut. Words start in the mouth, on the tongue, and at the teeth and lips. It is the breath that moves through the gut, filling the words with meaning and emotion."

Performers are primarily and passionately concerned with emotional truth. But we are not mimes. We need words to express our feelings. Without a deep conviction that words serve emotions, we overload the emotional response system and havoc, rather than passion, takes over.

Acting is convincing when the emotions are so deep inside the body that they seem to be essential and personal to that particular performer; when it is as though there were no outside world. This is subjective, visceral, inner, private acting. Having the technique to externalize these private emotions, to make them public *without* losing that personal connection to the text, is the performer's art.

3.

We evoke vibrations through the *placement* of vowels and consonants, the *physicality* of words, the *meaning* of words, and our *emotions* regarding that meaning.

WHAT IS PLACEMENT?

Placement is the way we keep words from getting jammed in the throat. Emotions tempt us to misplace the words; there is a witch's claw ready to snatch the vowels away from where they do us the most good.

Vowels and consonants have to have their special place on the tongue and at the lips and the teeth. Picture them bouncing on a freely moving tongue like a cork bobbing on the waves. The waves are not going to stop moving; the cork has to bob in its exact place. The trained body accepts this challenge so well that it can happen without the mind controlling the cork to keep it in place. This calls for spontaneity and precision.

COWBOY MOUTH

In Sam Shepard's wonderfully visceral play *Cowboy Mouth*, Slim screams, growls, and howls while Cavale, her throat hoarse from cigarettes and drink and physical exhaustion, yells him down.

How are we going to get through that performance without killing ourselves? Here we need placement, not for subtlety—more as a protection against what could be an occupational disaster.

The words in *Cowboy Mouth* come up from the body and are shaped by how the gut twists as it feels them; the emotional source of the word is somewhere in the body—wherever the emotion connected to the thought happens to land. In a deep structured joining, the breath bonds emotions to the words.

When the voice drops back in the throat there is little amplification and no resonance. It takes a lot of energy to talk from the throat.

Inexperienced performers pay little attention to placement. They make no connection between bad placement and a crude sound that frustrates characterization or between bad placement and fatigue and laryngitis. At first, they fear that practicing placement will be terribly boring. John Cage said that if something is boring try it twice; if it's still boring try it four times. Still boring? . . . eight, sixteen times . . . after a while it's not boring.

PHYSICALITY

HOW ARTICULATION AFFECTS AND REFLECTS OUR EMOTIONS

There is a quality of speech which makes us feel alive when we're acting, when the ah's and oh's — all the vowels — and the m's and v's and all the other consonants and all their combinations reward us with vibrations. Without vibrations words are boring, thin, they all sound alike; speaking without vibrations is eating lunch before the novocaine has worn off.

Words are exciting and as much a source of emotion as interpretation is. When filled with the emotion that the breath lays in them they are sensuous. Vibrations inhabit whatever complex response we have in our acting. When we feel vibrations we feel strong; our mental and physical energy is continuously renewed. Mostly, performers use words only as an outline to be filled in at some later date with a box of emotional Crayola.

Physicality refers to the energy and texture and uniqueness of each letter in a word. The actress said: "If I really know the scene, the words will come out with emotion." Not so. That's making the imagination do all the work. The actress had no sense of sound as a source of energy and feeling in and of itself.

Not being aware of the difference between the shape of each vowel and the texture of each consonant is like the chef not caring about the difference between cabbage and brussels sprouts. Each, more or less, could fit in the recipe.

The first and easiest way to get into the physical life of

the word is to know that the consonant B is different from D. V is different from Z. F...SH, M...N. AY is different from AH...Each letter vibrates, has a life of its own within the word.

Separate the sounds only in an exercise. Don't separate them in speaking hoping to *really* feel them. That's trying too hard.

THE USE OF THE VOWEL

Vowels are the strength and structure of words.

If the audience is jarred by a vowel sound alien to the speech of the character, it momentarily loses its belief in the character.

In the second scene of *Hamlet*, Laertes respectfully asks the king's permission to go to France:

> **KING CLAUDIUS:** And now, Laertes, what's the news with you?....
> What would'st thou have, Laertes?
>
> **LAERTES:** Dread my lord,
> Your leave and favor to return to France;...
> From whence though willingly I came to Denmark,
> To show my duty in your coronation,...

Laertes, personable and well-favored, stands on ceremony with an easy agreeableness. He is comfortable in his class privilege. The actor appreciated the psychological portrait of Laertes but couldn't convey the sound of ease, of confidence. He couldn't achieve the polish and poise of Laertes or elongate a vowel without seeming affected. When vowels are in their full size and rightful shape *they* give the character a natural rhythm and elegance in an unaffected and unadorned manner.

The actor had to study the vowels as if they were music,

giving the pronoun, MY, for example, two counts (MAH EE); the pronoun IT one count (IHT). Take note that the first two consonants in the word "whence" are WH, not W. Words that are spelled with a WH combination need the extra breath. The actor had to resist the temptation to tighten his tongue in his efforts to elongate the vowel. To elongate is to allow a vowel its full duration. A vowel pressed down on the tongue can't move. Released from pressure, allowed to move on its own, the vowel has beauty and simplicity. If the words adhere lightly to the blade of the tongue, there is the space between the tongue and the hard palate where they resonate.

Words have to touch the blade of the tongue. They do not hover above the tongue. That would be like a pianist playing the piano without touching the keys.

4.

THE TONGUE

We can't talk about talking without talking about the awesome power of the tongue. We taste food, speak, make love, and lick stamps with it. We experience a script sensuously through the words as we taste them on the blade of the tongue. Think of a full fat tongue, generous, like the breast of a nursing mother. Most performers are hardly aware of the tongue unless they are flubbing the words.

The tongue has direct access to the brain. Tongue and brain evolved together. The tongue is a muscular organ that obeys thought. Once it gets the message, we let it do the talking. The thought stays with what we say but the tongue says it.

In its biological intelligence, the tongue can take whatever shape is necessary to serve our needs. I eat a banana and I have no idea how my tongue moves.

A bad performance need not be bad for psychological reasons alone. It can also come from pounding the words onto the tongue. If we hit a K or a T too hard, or say them in an ineffective place in the mouth, for that fraction of a second we have jarred our psyche and impeded the flow of emotion. Below the conscious mind, when we accumulate too many of these bumps, we become distracted. To compensate, we try harder. And only make it worse.

ABOUT MEANING AND EMOTION BEING *IN* THE WORD

Elia Kazan, in his book *A Life*, quotes a director who doesn't want the performer to take so much time "thinking his thoughts. Think as you speak," said the director. That is a perfect way to describe what this chapter is about. The thought is in the words. The script's subtext has to be embedded in the actual words of the text.

The word that jumps ahead of the thought is meaningless. And taking too much time to insure the thought creates a gap between the performer and the character. We have also to be aware that it is possible to speak words without thinking the thoughts — a dangerous habit.

5.

Why are we bland about using words but act up a storm when it comes to our emotions? How is it that the vitality of speech has been lost?

Acting is a physical process. We feel in the gut what we think. Those physical feelings spill into words when we can no longer keep them inside. Acting and speaking may have to be taught separately but they are inseparable. How we feel is revealed in how we sound. Acting is Speaking.

When Did We Lose It, Where Did It Go?

In the turbulent 1960s we threw out language. Experimental theater groups distrusted the beautiful voice with the cultured mid-Atlantic vowels. They considered establishment plays irrelevant. Performers were into the body and yogic breathing and an acting style unfettered by traditional techniques. They were athletic and political. Content and movement were stressed over how the voice was produced or words delivered.

But there was a high energy in the work. The performers were committed to the artistic and political concerns of their productions; they believed in sharing, in *communication.*

The simplest kind of communication is being loud enough to be heard. The old chestnut is still relevant: "The ones in the balcony..." Speaking too softly debilitates energy. We must not get so lost in our feelings, submerging our emotions, having so private an experience that there is no communication going forth to others. Asked to speak louder, performers feel their emotional processes interrupted. Trying to reestablish contact, they literally lift their words away from the body. Stretching physically away from the self, from private emotions, is the last thing we want. Nothing rings true if we do not bring the psyche along with the body into our acting.

We are in the decade of the nineties. The energy of the sixties is past; the words that were thrown out have not come back. We jettisoned words because we believed they had lost passion and truth. They had become stale. But we may have thrown the baby out with the eloquence.

Richard Wilbur, the American Poet Laureate, in a TV interview:

> Some fundamental damage was done to our

national feeling for the language during the great troubles of the 1960s–early 1970s. There were so many young people who began all their sentences with "like" and broke up all their sentences with "y'know" and were being very scornful of eloquence. They thought that anything eloquent, anything adequate to what was under discussion, must be dishonest, phony, artificial. I, too, believe in sincerity but that period in which so many people were mistrustful of anybody or anything well said, well spoken, is something from which we have never recovered.

6.

We're not learning effortless speech just to please the audience. What matters even more is how it affects the performer. A release from tension allows the imagination its full scope to roam. We find subtleties of interpretation we could not otherwise have tapped into. We are like a player piano playing the music that our imagination created.

If there is no passion to communicate through language, if there is no awareness that language shapes emotion, that vowels and consonants are a sensual response to the script, it is as though a pall is cast over the whole performance. Instinctively, the audience is waiting for the high that comes from feeling the performer's vibrations. If vibrations are missing, they get a performance — but no cigar.

SUMMING UP

An audience *can* read thoughts. Silence *can* resonate with meaning. Robert De Niro, as a priest in *True Confessions*, is a guest at lunch in an exclusive restaurant. Something is said that the priest finds disturbing. He suppresses his answer.

But we can see his emotions as they pass over his face as clearly as we watch clouds reflected on the glass facade of a high-rise building. De Niro's acting has a deep interior power.

But there are roles in which body language alone will not serve a performer, not even De Niro. As Louis Cypher, the devil Lucifer, in *Angel Heart*, he is first seen sitting, majestic, his hair glistening smooth and drawn back as though he were in an eighteenth-century drawing room, hands poised artfully on his cane, his fingernails eerie. He could not complete the characterization because he did not bring that same elegance into his speech. His speech was inappropriate to his otherwise stylized behavior.

Some performers work only from the body; some only from analysis. It's all important — analysis, psychology, words, breath, body, charisma, vibes, imaging . . . Nothing is purely mental. Nothing is merely physical.

VIBRATIONS

Vibrations occur when breath, mind, gesture, and word are in sync. It's as though intuition glides along a rope-ladder of vibrations and we tap into deeper responses to the material. When we are integrated, mind inside body, we mean what we say, do what we mean to do, and mean what we do.

Imagine two pianos, one a Steinway Grand and the other a child's toy. One produces vibrations, the other a little tinny sound. We can play Beethoven's Piano Sonata on the Steinway but not on the toy piano. Acting Hamlet while speaking the words in the back part of the mouth (which is not a vibrating area) is like playing the Sonata on the child's piano.

≈≈≈

When the breath is not brought all the way up through the mouth to the word there are no vibrations.

When the words hover above instead of touching the blade of the tongue — no vibrations.

When we grab at sounds in the throat, we feel misleading vibrations.

The tongue has to be free of tension; it has to feel large and alive and willing to accept the words we give it to speak; the tongue needs a sense of humor.

The inside of the mouth has to be a lively, changing space. The mouth is the body's busiest center, a depot into which the breath has flowed carrying thoughts and emotional responses, and from which the tongue moves it all out in the shape of words to share with the audience.

≈≈≈

When vibrations occur, we feel centered. There is a bonding between our internal impulses and our external actions. Only after this initial bonding can we bond with the audience.

We instinctively sense another person's vibrations. We experience and identify with their vibrations, give and receive emotional messages. Not only others, we turn ourselves on by our vibrations. If my tongue has vibrations I can't help but be influenced by the energy that I feel. I gain assurance from the confidence in my own voice. Vibration is energy. The audience loves the performer whose mental and physical energy fits like a glove.

Vibrations come from below the rational mind; from the breath and the tongue interacting with words. They rise up from the blade of the tongue like steam from the sidewalk on a hot day, like bubbles from poured milk. No disconnections. We have to know *physically* what it means "to live in those vibrations" because living in vibrations is what we do when we act.

3

LETTING THE BODY
DO IT ALSO

1.

When the mind moves away from the body, it becomes unduly aware of itself. It begins to distrust, to censor, to lose confidence. There is no support system. Fear enters whenever there is a break in the integration of mind, word, and gesture.

How do we integrate these forces? Through the breath. The breath is a god-like messenger that moves through the space of the body keeping every part in touch with every other part.

2.

Most of us have to learn how to breathe before we can recognize a compressed breath in the body. That compression, that little death, makes us try harder because we feel that something is wrong and we don't know what it is.

When the mind alone makes associations, these translate into a limited number of mannered reactions, gestures in stock, like items from the old Sears Roebuck catalogue. In the opera, Carmen sashaying around the stage with her hands on her hips convinces no one, least of all herself, that she is sexy. Carmen's sexuality, odd as it may sound, is in a moving jaw hinge and her full, fat tongue. Sensuality flourishes in the cells of the body, in the gums inside the mouth, the breath. The actor playing Stanley Kowalski follows his breath which carries his desire and sexuality into the deepest part of his torso. If the actor disconnects from the breath, he is disconnected from desire and flexing his pumped-up muscles makes him no more than a jock.

The psychology of character, style, meaning is in the

body, the tongue, the breath, and the imagination. The imagination and the soul find shelter in the body.

Meryl Streep and Jack Nicholson seem to have nothing in their bodies that obstructs the way they reveal character. Streep in *Heartburn* plays a darling daughter who leaves her philandering husband and goes back to Daddy, who lives in New York. When she walks down Broadway, the audience sees how Streep has absorbed the character right down into her legs. Privileged girls on the Upper West Side walk like that. In the movie *Ironweed*, Nicholson's character, an alcoholic derelict, sitting in an abandoned lot around a fire is disturbed by a memory. His rage takes over, and we see it immediately in a terrifying thrust of his clenched fist. His fist was the outward part of his rage.

Think of Wild Child, that creature of myth brought up outside of society, who is physical and emotional but neither educated nor socialized. It's hard to recognize these elemental qualities today. We are so influenced by psycho-cultural considerations that our immediate response to physical intelligence seems to have been lost.

For most people, the sensuous life is only in sexuality. But sensuousness is in our lives minute by minute. A performer who can reorder priorities to include working from the body finds that its rewards are sumptuous. Joseph Campbell, in his talks with Bill Moyers, exhorts us to experience life on the purely physical plane. Campbell calls it the "rapture of life." Wild Child experiences it. Performers, searching for "meaning," often miss the rapture.

3.

Like archeologists on a dig, we have to feel our way starting at the surface with the words; descending deeper into the body, we use all the senses and not too much of the calculating mind. The archeologist who has no rhythm, intuition, or sensuality won't feel the shard under the fingers. That's what performers are groping for — the shards of passion or memory or knowledge. We want to be alert with half-closed eyes, to trust and to act from, in addition to psychological analysis, of course, the emotional signals that the body sends.

Body language, however subtle, communicates clearly once we learn to hear it. That is why the disciplines of Tai Chi and the Alexander Technique are so useful — if we have the patience to study until we understand what we are being taught. The Tai Chi master uses few words. The meaning is in the accumulated movements of Tai Chi. What a performer *does* in those *movements* gathers together into an understanding. The Alexander teacher, inculcating awareness of and release from tensions, conveys meaning by touching the body. The words are in the touch. It is from the years of feeling the teacher's touch that we understand.

What does rhythm feel like? Rhythm is not only what we hear from a five-piece band. The body has its own natural rhythm. It rises to the surface when the barricades erected by tension are removed. Rhythm is what feels *appropriate;* the movement of a breeze over grass, nothing planned, things moving in ways slightly different from each other but with an uninterrupted, harmonious balance. I inhale the scent of jasmine from my neighbor's garden on a hot night. That is one kind of rhythm for me. Having butterflies on opening night is another.

When we put undue effort into our emotional reactions, press too hard in the muscle, control, "act" too much, we can't feel the inner rhythm because it can't get through the blockage. Let it be. A faint signal goes a long way.

When ideas are not folded into the breath performers are overwhelmed by theory and explanation and become serious, obedient, and academic. We must give up "trying to get it right" and do the work with some pleasure. Don't mistake sentimentality for pleasure. There is a good physical feeling in breathing before we speak or gesture. It is not putting a half smile on the face, it's something in the body, deep down in the breath. It *feels good* to release tension in the tongue, it *feels good* to speak words that are not trapped in the throat, and it *feels good* to feel the lightness of movement when we move on the breath.

And when all is said, some days we're better off acting with some tension than worrying about not having released it.

TRUSTING IN THE BODY

Why do we move fluidly in daily life and awkwardly in performance? We seem to interfere with simple actions the most. After his big hit playing Charlie Chaplin, Robert Downey Jr. said that he had had trouble doing the simple things, like walking to the door or picking up the phone. In life, reading the paper, for example, something catches our attention, we give it a glance, and go on reading. But when we act, the glance may become too big. And it is usually followed by a grimace or a tightening of the shoulders. In his only scene in a movie, a young actor had to cross to the door. After a few steps, he gestured unnecessarily; he scratched his arm. He couldn't get body and psyche together to make that cross. This is a performer's equivalent to an Olympic runner's ten-second sprint. It takes about the same amount of preparation and dedication.

It's odd that we don't trust the body when we act. We make sure it will do what we want by controlling it. If we controlled our lovemaking to do it right we'd have to go to a shrink.

A good lover is perceptive,
A good lover gets information from the body,

A good lover doesn't overtalk it.
A good performer likewise.

4.

Athletes talk about getting the mind out of the way so
that Something can take over. The athlete said: "I can't concentrate when I think." The body has to be let alone to do
whatever it does, its own way.

≈≈≈

And the saboteur of all this freedom and expressiveness
is:

TENSION.

For ten years a drummer had held his drumsticks so
tightly and beat the drums so furiously that one day he
showed signs of hand deterioration so debilitating and
painful it seemed he would never drum again. He had to
hold his hands in a bucket of freezing water immediately after performance. He had to retrain himself to hold the
drumsticks lightly. Through painstaking changes in his
technique, he was able, finally, to hold his sticks in such a
way that lightness in doing became a natural response. It
takes guts to practice the way he did.

The actress could feel vibrations from the words in her
throat. When she spoke from the front half of her face,
however, it felt too light — as though nothing was happening. Will she practice again and again until "lightly doing"
is natural and desirable?

THE UNSUSTAINABLE LIGHTNESS OF BEING AND DOING

When I'm learning something new I tend to squeeze on
my breath and press on the back of my tongue or my ribs.
My muscles should have no extra pressure from me. They

should do only the contracting and releasing that nature intended. When I'm rehearsing and feel stress, I stop and exhale. I feel the air moving over the lower lip. This helps me
to calm down. Then, lightly thinking of my intentions in the
scene I access the words and actions and hope for the best.

Why is it so hard to give up working hard? We perceive
heaviness as reliable. It is hard to trust the delicacy, the
lightness of a faint impulse, a fleeting thought, an easily spoken word, and a weightless gesture.

5.

It's hard to be interested in this muscles talk if we're unable to feel the quirks and peculiarities we have acquired
through the habitual misuse of the Self. It is the body causing mischief. The body is mysterious:

> On a clear day you can barely grab your ass
> with both hands.
>   Old Saying

To speak we tighten the lips and move the eyebrows.
Not very logical. It happens when we feel that something is
wrong and compensate by tiny haphazard corrections and
end by throwing all the parts of our body out of alignment.
In time, the body loses the impulse for natural, ongoing
movement.

We place our secrets of fear, anxiety, inferiority, self-
consciousness, and the double whammy of "trying to be
good" in the back teeth, the jaw hinge, shoulders, the rib
cage, the soles of the feet... at least two thousand places.
What's the use of counting — except for our eyelashes and
earlobes, we tighten all over the body. Some of the worst
body tensions are:

- the tight tongue
- stiffness in the back of the neck

- in the toes ... the big toe
- in the shoulders ...

Muscular tension anywhere in the body can spoil a performance.

It takes time to recognize habitual tension. Then it takes time to learn how to release it. And then it takes time to learn new behavior. And it's hard to make changes: "Don't take away what I have ... even though it's not doing me any good. I don't care who I will be later — I can barely deal with who I am now." We need time to allow ourselves to fail until we succeed.

Tension has to be continually released. A muscle can start out being free and become tense as we go through the day. We have to be careful not to keep ourselves so busy that we don't notice it building up. In class the actress was walking strangely. Her ankles were inflexible and her toes were stiff. She had no breath, and nothing seemed to move. We had to stop and examine her daily routine to find her hidden agenda. Her days and nights were filled with meetings, writing sessions, her boyfriend's performance, the picture session with her agent, the video tapes to look at ... Everything leading to her work was taking the place of the work. There was no space left for art. Her life was ruled by the "right career moves." Art needs empty time and empty space without schedules and goals.

≈≈≈

Bad habits numb physical feelings. We ignore body signals because we are unaware that we are receiving them; fear is buried in the body structure and it has frozen the muscle. Then we disconnect. We have to give the brain and body a chance to figure out a new technique, a chance to coordinate and integrate with it. Although nature has provided us with the tools — we can breathe and move — awareness is missing. When the quiet mind "sees and understands first," the muscles have, in a sense, rehearsed the action.

> Thought is a rehearsal for action.
> — Albert Einstein

WHAT HAS TENSION TO DO WITH ACTING?

We make believe the script is real. Our imagination influences the body and then the body makes the make-believe really real. The imagination needs the body to show and tell. If there are roadblocks of tension in the body, there is no through-traffic of ideas. We clear the body of emotional debris, of muscle tension, in order to let it have open channels to receive thoughts and images that serve the acting impulse.

ZOMBIE ACTING

At first performers find the idea of releasing tension in their acting to be threatening. An actor wondered, "if it won't make us zombie actors?" When his face was contorted he felt he was really emotional.

The body will do its work of reflecting emotions. In great anger the muscle will contract greatly. We don't need to add to it. Putting pressure on the muscle over and beyond what the task requires is the beginning of Overacting. It's a Catch-22. At the same time that performers worry about being zombies they worry about being too big in their responses. So they hold back. Underacting is not good acting. Neither is contorting the face to show emotion.

Summing Up

An idea can get trapped in the body so that we are unable to do what we mean to do. A thought can get trapped in strangled articulation so that we are unable to say what we mean. We can act with tension but the performance doesn't come out the way we meant it. It's like trying to talk on the telephone with a lousy connection. Tension doesn't allow a performance to grow larger and more flowing; it diminishes emotional response. We get caught in a landscape of tight muscles trying to express terror or suffering. We are in a double bind; we have pulled up the bridge to the body, locking out emotions. Then we fake it.

Don't misplace power. The source of power is in two places: in thought and breath. No amount of muscle pressure can substitute for them.

4

LEARNING HOW TO LEARN

1.

I found a letter that I wrote and never sent to my students. It was after class and late at night:

My darling students, we are in a terrible state. You are coming to acting class frozen stiff with fear and over-motivation and you are so preoccupied with judging and evaluating your talent that you can't do the simplest exercise. It's time to learn how to learn.

You feel your talent a vague shape inside you. When you receive a technique you obsess on it and learn it in only one way. You think the rules will help you to shape and define this talent. You're confusing technique with control. As soon as you do this, you bring your talent into a static condition. Instead of handling it better, you feel yourself losing it little by little.

Finally you clear a path out of that jumble of emotions you were trying to express and what happens? You've lost the sense of character you had. You've lost the rhythm you intuited. You learned too correctly, you overcorrected your mistakes. Now you can move but you forget why you are moving. And, finally convinced that a performer must have more than three notes in the voice, you're stuck with range but no meaning.

Those performers who don't apply themselves to learning technique keep their vanity happy but lose effectiveness. They feel but can't express. They are sloppy. They have no sense of structure. Those who try to learn technique lose their rhythm, their spontaneity. An actor said: "I don't know how to feel free anymore." Technique is liberating. It just doesn't seem like it at first.

Where does the ego go while you are learning? You are left feeling helpless, small, and ego-less. And Ego, stuffed away somewhere, grows monstrously out of proportion, scratching for success. You have lost ego and become totally egotistical. You must find a balanced ego, maintaining a sense of self while feeling part of the process, being able to surrender to the rules of the art. Working with detachment (admittedly a confusing concept at first) helps to achieve a balance between caring and not-caring.

Our culture demands instant gratification and instant results. Anything that doesn't make you sound natural immediately, from the first lesson, is somehow defective. It doesn't matter if in the end you will really sound natural — "if the first lesson doesn't feel natural, drop it." That's a great mistake.

About preparation: you can, with one thought, release tension in the body when thirty minutes of warm-up have done nothing for you. I've seen kids kill the instinct of acting by over-preparation. They pause, concentrate, loosen the arms, and finally perform a dull monologue. That's because the pause wasn't really a pause, the shake of the arms was mechanical, the concentration was fear.

There are countless ways to betray yourself. You've got to keep the body supple, free of tension. But all the exercise in the world won't help if the mind is tight and frightened. That brings us once again to attitude, to a philosophy of life, career, art...

And there the letter ends. It was pretty late by then to deal with the philosophy of life and art.

Performers all have pretty much the same hangups. They erect barriers between themselves and the techniques they set out to learn, mostly by trying too hard. Then they become wary of technique. But the techniques are not the problem. The barriers are the problem. It's hard to keep eagerness at bay. Eagerness is a natural response but it doesn't serve the art.

Magic Johnson in his book *My Life* talks about playing basketball when he was a kid:

> I wanted to be good, so I practiced and played constantly. As hard as my father worked on his job, I worked on the basketball court. But I always found a way to make it fun. When I was alone, I'd play imaginary full court games...I'd be (Wilt) Chamberlain going one way and (Dave) Bing going the other.

By the time Magic was playing professional basketball he had practiced with pleasure for so long that his muscles remembered and retained the feeling. Confidence and exuberance were embedded in his body and psyche.

If we study with anxiety and impatience, that is the feeling we take into performance. Work at it and let it alone. Playfulness is necessary for learning. A scientific study observed young animals playing recklessly and dangerously. The scientists concluded that evolution would not have allowed such feats were they not essential for the maturing process.

A Fairy Tale
The Very Beginning
The Hag and the Performer

The Performer adores the Golden Bird of Acting and sets out through the dense Forest to win it with help from the Old Hag. Astride the Hag, the Performer whips her on: "Faster. Faster. Why are you taking so long?" The Hag replies, "You don't see the traps laid for us. It is your confusion and misconception entangled in the roots and branches and vines that is taking the time. Not I."

The Performer huffs and puffs for a moment and then: "All right, all right, have it your way... but let's GET ON WITH IT!" And they continue on their Journey.

When we set out to learn we must STOP TIME.

Don't study with an eye to the casting agents and producers. It's important to know when we're ready for which part of the acting experience. We should be like children playing a game when we learn. When children play, nothing interferes with the game.

2.

The desire to perform is very great but it is often mixed in with self-consciousness and embarrassment. A part of the body shrinks back from its own presence; there is a pulling away from a gesture as soon as it's made. Words are withdrawn into the back of the mouth where they get trapped. The mind saying one thing and the body saying the opposite means mixed messages are being sent. Neither performer nor audience believes them. In the early lessons it's necessary to stop as soon as an exercise gets cluttered with Little Grabs:

- Straightening up to sit properly
- Toes rigid, the big toe especially
- Shoulders shifting slightly
- The back of the neck thrusting the chin forward
- Ankles making little half circles
- Cord in the neck showing
- Throbbing at the temples...

(Add your own if you don't find it listed.)

3.

If we let the critic in us take over, it will eventually paralyze us. There is a place in the body, an actual place, that each person's critic inhabits and which smothers natural talent. It's what happens just before we start the exercise — the "Uh oh, now I have to do it" response: clearing the throat, twitching the elbows like a hen getting ready to lay an egg: "It's acting time and I have to be perfect." Those little grabs.

We can learn to recognize a barely noticeable tension that is brought on by a slight mental discomfort. Pressing down in the body, we leave a healthy working attitude and cross into a remembered stress behavior.

Like many of my performer friends who moved from New York to Los Angeles and had to learn to drive, I was so scared of merging onto the freeway that I couldn't tell which lane I was in as I looked over my left shoulder. My fear had locked off something in my brain. Performers interfere with their naturally intelligent responses to an exercise in the same way:

One actress is nervous when she begins the exercise. Her eyes blink and she doesn't quite hear what she's supposed to do. Another actor starts an improvisation by jutting his chin forward; this not only locks off his breath, it inhibits the flow of his images. One of the singers begins every aria by putting a sentimental expression in his eyes. Another actress feels the pounding in her heart. She worries "what her friends in the industry will think."

When we care too much, or try too hard, we can't even understand what the exercise calls for. By putting pressure in the body, somewhere, anywhere, we stop the breath from moving; the mind separates from the exercise and the acting that we do from that point on has nothing to do with our talent. We force ourselves to finish the exercise but we don't really mean any of it.

Don't Open The Store For Business — and then shut the doors and pull down the window shades.

Learn how to get helpful feedback from the body. If we can feel a tightness in the chest which inhibits our acting, we can also feel an openness which allows the breath to flow freely to serve our acting.

About Ego

An actor in a voice class was using the Blah Blah syllable. He resisted using it. He needed the class but didn't consider it advanced enough.

One actress admitted always wanting to be The Best. This leads to a harrowing self-criticism. The only way she could wean herself from the habit was to stay with the techniques, going from one feeling to the next.* Ain't nobody said it was going to be easy. Acting, arguably, is easy. *Learning* to act is hard.

Another actress had the "smart" problem in a more subtle way. She couldn't permit herself to look dumb. Being

---

* The words "feelings" and "emotions" are sometimes interchangeable. Every emotion has a physical counterpart, which we experience dimly or strongly. Or don't or can't experience; it exists in the body, nonetheless. I use the word "feeling" in the physical sense: cold or hot air on the skin, a paper cut, the breath moving through the torso, the words on the blade of the tongue. I think of "emotion" as belonging to the imagination.

smart — being quick to catch on — isn't part of our learning life. It really doesn't matter. Art crosses all lines. There is no sophistication or social status when we study acting. The only time a gesture might seem ungainly, or the Blah Blah syllable sound foolish, is when we inhibit the exercise.

Watch that ego. It's the thirteenth witch who wasn't invited to the party.

OUT OF THE FOREST INTO THE CLEARING

...And So... The Hag and the Performer, technique by technique, work their way out of the Forest into the Clearing. They approach the Castle where the Golden Bird is waiting to be released. Now the Hag must stay below while the Performer begins the long, lonely climb up to the tower. Reaching the first balcony, the Performer is eager to push on. But the Hag shouts Reminders: "Step by Step! Eagerness is Ego! Ego — NO! — don't make sure! Don't hold your breath!! Be nice to the guards on the way up — you never know who you'll meet coming down!"

And the Performer stops, remembers to breathe, and step by step and hand over hand climbs up the Castle Wall.

4.

Thoughts that flit into the mind which waste time:

- Am I holding the teacher up?
- This doesn't feel like acting.
- This technique is harder than I thought.
- I'm not getting it.
- All my friends are doing scenes already.
- I should know this by now, what's wrong with me?
- I got it right the last lesson. I gotta get it right again.

With this attitude, one does the exercise with determination mingled with despair.

When we get right down to it, connecting breath, word, and thought is not just an exercise; add character and story, and it becomes performance.

AT LAST

...Squeezing in through the little window, the Performer grabs hold of the Bird, never, never to let go — but the Hag's warning from below is Shrill: "If you don't let go, the Bird will die." Just in time the Performer releases the chokehold, remembers the Technique and finger-trains the Bird. The Bird is free. Free to fly and free to perch. After which the Bird sings its song. Most of the time.

≈≈≈

The Performer: "I can't find the words to thank you."

The Hag: "Never mind the words, dear. Just find the ducats."

≈≈≈

To explain a technique I hold out my two hands.

"It's this way." (I show my one hand.)

"No. It's this way." (I show the other hand.)

"It's a little of this and a little of the opposite. Well, actually, it's neither the one nor the other. It's this:"

I hold my hands together and there is a tiny crack between them. "It's in that tiny space. It is mysterious and inexplicable and *we find it for ourselves* — any which way we can."

≈≈≈

What seems like contradictory instruction is confusing.

But being a true believer and holding on to one way of learning because we're scared to let go is dangerous. There are no guarantees. We can't write "art" down in a notebook and memorize it.

True, we can really mess up an exercise by not being watchful enough. But messing up isn't permanent. Being too careful, on the other hand, is pernicious. Even with its attendant insecurity it's better to dare, to take a chance and see what the exercise and, for that matter, what acting is like without that control.

Most of us can't start at the beginning, at Zero. That's too advanced. We have to work our way up to Zero. Zero is simplicity. Zero is nothing but what is there. A performer may bring to the lessons a hidden agenda of self-doubt, old mistaken notions, family anger... If the ground before Zero is not cleared of psychological resistance we cannot hear what is being said. Psychological resistance creates physical tension. Scared muscles make learning a little harder.

Some performers prefer to dwell on tales of their victimization rather than getting on with the exercise. Let's not get hung up on the hangups. In the recording of his talks with the two-thousand-year-old man, Carl Reiner asks Mel Brooks, the World Famous Psychiatrist, how he was able to cure Bernice, the lady who couldn't stop tearing paper all day. The World Famous Psychiatrist replies that he explained to her that "it wasn't nice, a nice girl like her, she should sit around all day in the house tearing paper. So she stopped."

5.

We want to learn our craft in such a way that there is no need, ever, to unlearn it.

The study of acting should be benign. Acting lessons are not a battle. We evolve into being performers, we don't get there through jarring the psyche or fearing the teacher or fearing to make a mistake. But a teacher standing over us and telling us what to do and what not to do makes us feel self-concious at the same time that we are supposed to relax and be uninhibited. It is another Catch-22. However, if we have witnessed bad acting and heard hollow voices, we know acting cannot "just happen," and we recognize that we must learn the techniques that correct such mistakes.

6.

THE STEP-BY-STEP METHOD

We are all hooked on wanting to perform (otherwise known as being result-oriented). But we have to be taught process, because there is no other way to learn.

Being result-oriented means:

- Tying a shoelace before one's foot is entirely in the shoe.
- Worrying in Act I about Act III where we have the big emotional scene.
- Worrying about performance during rehearsal.

In an improvisation, Mary is sitting with legs crossed. Jane asks Mary to type a report. Before Mary *hears* Jane ask, she uncrosses her legs to go to the typewriter.

Be careful to not hear too carefully. In life, our timing is usually perfect. We hear, we do.

Being result-oriented has nothing to do with talent or intelligence. Most of us start out by grabbing at results. It is embedded in our culture. (We can always blame the culture.) But the best performers have learned to respond to what is going on in the scene minute by minute.

THE DO-NOTHING METHOD

The do-nothing is important. Imagine an oval, an empty space in the mind. When suggestions are made, suspend the impulse to do something. Put the suggestions in that empty space.

THE 1, 2, 3 METHOD

I worked with an actress who had no confidence; she was nervous about everything from scene work to the simplest exercise. She either jumped ahead of what she really felt or took too long because she tried too hard. But she could count 1, 2, 3, putting nothing in between the numbers. And that is how the 1, 2, 3 Method evolved.

The 1, 2, 3 way is to hear, have a thought, respond. I'm talking nanoseconds. When the count is: $1 \ldots$ uh $\ldots 1\frac{1}{2}$, $2 \ldots$ uh $\ldots 2\frac{3}{4}$, that is mental interference, and it shows lack of confidence.

Let's take a breathing exercise:

- Breathing out on an F consonant = 1.
- The air coming back in by itself = 2.
- Breathing out again on an F = 3.

Extend the exercise to include a sound:

- Breathing out on the F consonant = *1*.
- The air coming back in and up to the syllable = 2.
- Saying BLAH = 3.
- Count out loud:
- *1, 2, 3*. Simplicity. Don't let anything come between the numbers other than breath, if that is necessary.

When I first started using 1, 2, 3 I didn't realize how

useful it would be. The 1, 2, 3 Method can be fast, medium, slow; we can take what ever time is needed as long as we keep a rhythm.

1.......2.......3 or

1....2....3 or

1..2..3 or

1.2.3.

Hear.......breathe.......speak

Hear....breathe....speak

Hear..breathe..speak

Hear.breathe.speak.

It isn't as if Moses came down from the mountain bearing this command along with the other ten. I write "hear — breathe" but perhaps it is "breathe — hear." Once we begin to work with breath, the body will do it its way. We each make our own discoveries.

ACT and *then* analyze. When an exercise is over, put on the Lab Coat and consider what needs to be done differently.

THE LAB-COAT ATTITUDE

Let us suppose I am the Nobel Prize-winning Scientist and the performer is my Brilliant Young Researcher. We have put on our lab coats and are making determinations regarding an ongoing research project: the *Feeding Formula for Guppies*. Once a week, followed by my BYR taking notes, I inspect the fish tanks.

Tank 1 — all the fish have died. I change the formula.

Tank 2 — half are gone. I delay a decision.

Tank 3 — the fish are thriving and having baby guppies.

The Brilliant Young Researcher, although passionately

involved in the experiment, is not filled with self-reproach because the experiment did not work in two of the tanks. It is not looked upon as a personal failure and, *sotto voce*, good-bye Sweden. Instead, observant and objective, the Brilliant Young Researcher continues to make changes until the right formula is found and, as a matter of fact, becomes pretty good at sprinkling the exact number of grains of fish food into the tanks.

Performers reproach themselves and consider the failure of an exercise a reflection of their talent, whereas they should be discovering the parameters of the exercise. How many mistakes are needed before there are no more to be made?

Stay calm. Keep the attention on the exercise and keep out the emotional junk waiting like a sporozoite to settle down on some cozy host cell in the brain.

Don't take it personally.

ABOUT WORKSHOPS

When we have a track record of good performances, and something new has to be learned, it's easier to say: "How does that go? Show me." When there is no track record, the concern is that people won't recognize our real talent. Have no fear. Talent is spotted even when we are at our clumsiest.

Feeling good about oneself as a performer is very important. Taking a workshop in "The Joy Of..." is useful. But without the techniques of speech, gesture, and imagery, I've never seen anyone become a better performer by talking about personal feelings.

Some performers do fine in acting workshops but many compound their difficulties. If we are too eager to play ball with the big kids, we will begin to use the body and voice in ways that are harmful to us.

The most time- and cost-effective way to begin study is in private lessons or, if they are ongoing, small classes. When we are ready for it, a workshop offers a place to meet other performers and bounce good ideas around regarding play analysis and characterization. We learn to compete in an exciting rational way. Before entering a Workshop we need detailed lessons in:

Breathing.

The release of tension.

Awareness of overcorrecting, grabbing, trying too hard.

Summing Up

Students feel frustrated when they prepare elaborately before a scene and then find all that truthfulness turning fake as soon as the acting begins. It's the good students who sometimes suffer the most. They hang on to what they have learned. Talent hides away somewhere, away from the *sturm und drang* and the angst and the pull of career goals — all that *striving*. Some say: "Don't study. Lessons will screw you up." They will only if we take instruction too literally.

≈≈≈

If we let what we learn seep down below our consciousness, below what we think of as rock bottom, it will seem as if acting just happens to be something we are able to do, something we were born to do. Performers have to know their techniques so thoroughly that no outsider can spot them.

Acting is intuition joined with technique. Intuition is instinctive knowing and cannot be taught. Intuition comes to us mysteriously but leaves us mysteriously as well. Technique is the means by which we access intuition. Technique *can* be taught.

5

TECHNIQUE

*In India they lay a gold leaf on the food as it
is served. The gold leaf settles on the food for
a moment, we see it and then it becomes an
invisible ingredient. It was there. It has become a part of us but no one can locate it.*
— An Actor On Tour

1.

We want to dig a hole. With our two hands we begin.
We feel our limitations. We're stuck in one position, we
can't dig as large a hole as we imagined. We invent the
shovel. The shovel is an extension of our hand. Our hand is
an extention of our brain and our desire. Technique is an extension of ourselves.

As long as we keep it connected to the source, the
breath.

There has to be movement back and forth between the
source and technique, each sustaining the other.

Sometimes an empty space intervenes between the
performer-in-training and the artist. It is partly because
some of what we learn has to be learned in tiny segments,
and this tends to separate us from the larger concept. We
sometimes forget to integrate with the larger concept when
we reach performance. Practicing scales takes love, respect,
and humility, but when the pianist plays Chopin, it is not the
scales that are played. That has become a part of a trusted
technique. The pianist will play Chopin.

2.

THEORY refers to the ideal way; what we conceive acting to be. Theory involves understanding the point of it all, the principle. TECHNIQUE is the How To Do It. It is the step-by-step carrying out of the theory. We experience theory in the bones through technique.

≋≋≋

Performers are afraid of giving a cold, technical performance. It is a valid concern. An actor I worked with had been trained to speak with resonance and perfectly shaped vowels. He could stride upon the stage and was not afraid of gesturing. But he was a very private person; there was always a separation between what he felt and how he spoke. He avoided the deeper emotions. He made his voice and movements serve in their stead.

No matter how well-trained, if a performer is speaking words without emotional or intellectual commitment to their meaning, that is a cool performer giving a cold, technical performance. There are also hot performers who love the audience and would give their all to do a good show, who are nevertheless doing hack work and giving technical performances. The reason, oddly enough, is the same. Unwittingly, the hot performer has disconnected from the inner impulse and the acting has become exaggerated and unbelievable.

CELLULAR INTELLIGENCE

Performers don't believe that a technique will eventually work by itself. They forget cellular intelligence. We have to give the cells a chance to take the lessons, too. I watched myself take in food. My tongue uses the tip to lick ice cream, it sends steak to the molars for real chewing, it rounds itself in the middle, like a spoon, for soup. Past infancy and once learned, this is technique working by itself.

When we first learn we intrude into the material. Later we eliminate that split between thought and response — awareness without intrusion. For example: We wait for the green light to cross the street. We don't actually say, "Now it's green, I can cross." We are aware of it but we are not actively thinking it. It wasn't always like that. When we were kids, a parent held us by the hand and we got body signals that told us when to wait at the corner and when to cross. When we got old enough to go to school we were warned to wait for the green light and scolded if we ran into the street before it was safe. After we learned the lesson, we didn't hang on to the instruction. It was finally in our awareness. It is a matter of life or death, but we trust our awareness and cross the street according to some deeply-accepted training. Acting is no different.

3.

Technique takes the anxiety out of acting. Technique is the angelic guide to Spontaneity. What is spontaneity? We all mention it, desire it, take it for granted — but what, really, is it?

Spontaneity is 1, 2, 3 — nothing between the thought and the word. It is putting nothing between the impulse to move and the movement itself.

We can have spontaneity and technique, but we can't have spontaneity without technique.

MISTAKES ALMOST EVERYONE MAKES

Struggling to get technique we fail to communicate what the piece is about. When we let in the emotions, the muscles tighten up and we act without breath. When the emotions and the voice and the body are in sync, acting reflects what we think and feel.

A technique may not be immediately understood and

doable. Why should it be? Give the brain and the body a chance to figure it out, a chance to coordinate, to integrate. Don't start to work until a little moss grows on the rock. It has to do with eagerness. The singer would run to the practice room on his lunch hour. But he never allowed his breath to start properly, so he practiced without breath. He would have done less damage had he eaten a burger and fries and read the funny papers.

On the other hand, don't be timid. Just Do It.

≈≈≈

When we finally learn a technique, we want it to do wonders for us. "Take me where I most want to go," says the rider, flogging the horse. Under those conditions the horse will either die or unseat the rider. Rider and horse have to become one entity. They find a rhythm together. They communicate command and inclination to each other. The horse feels the subtle commands of the rider and the rider feels the inclinations of the horse. Mind and body. In sync.

4.

The very first technique we learn is to breathe out on an F consonant. This helps us release anxiety. But it's hard for some performers to believe that it matters. "Yeah, but... when I'm acting I don't want..." The performer is trying to make the technique invisible.

When we were kids and went to the movies, we saw on the screen what was magic to our eyes and passionately wanted that for ourselves. We think that feeling the air on the lower lip or finding the right weight for the exhale can't possibly have anything to do with real acting. So we skip all that stuff to get to what we think is performance. It takes many lessons to give up that dream and become fascinated by what lies underneath — the infrastructure of performance.

SUMMING UP

Sometimes, having learned a technique, the performer is saddled with a whole new set of mannerisms. It's enough to make the teacher miss a heartbeat. I've seen performers shake themselves out in the middle of a sentence, having been taught to keep the body free of tension. They behave as if they have a neurological disorder. It helps to think of technique as the absence of unnecessary actions.

Technique is nothing but redeeming natural behavior, getting rid of physical tensions, cleaning out emotional garbage. All this so that we can find our way back to simplicity. When we reclaim our innocence, the self without fear or exaggeration, we are talented and intuitive and imaginative and creative and integrated.

≈≈≈

Technique is not doing something.
Technique is doing nothing.

6

DOING NOTHING

1.

After he teaches Luke the techniques for using the light saber and after much practice, Obi Wan Kenobi tells Luke to use The Force; that now he must let go of his conscious self and act on instinct.

Do nothing. Receive.

We are afraid of doing nothing because we don't know what it means. To do nothing is to stop trying to do the right thing; to stop trying to use what has just been learned. It is a relief, sometimes, to stop trying so hard. Doing nothing is not forcing a thought into the mind. It is to have the courage to feel empty.

Think of receiving the breath, of receiving an idea, an inspiration.

We have a good angel that guides us during acting. It perches on the farthest circle of our awareness. In a performance, if there is trouble, the angel moves up closer to give benign advice. Doing nothing allows us to hear this super-quiet command.

The malicious angel is mental interference. It lives on the inner circle, too close to the performing. It's a talker.

≈≈≈

"OK, I'll do it a thousand times in order to learn it." "OK, I did it a thousand times, now give me what I want..." If desire is too close to the work, it's going to interfere. It's not that we have to be free of desire—we are contemporary American performers, after all; we are not taking an acting workshop in the Himalayan mountains. But desire placed too close to technique or performance tightens muscles and gets between us and the role, like sand in a sandwich. Intuition secretes itself when there are too many gestures, too much muscle activity, too much thinking. Doing nothing lets the intangible happen.

2.

We're told to follow the rules but not too literally. How do we cool down our conscientious effort, our zeal?

Suppose we were learning how to grow roses. Even though we may be getting instruction from *The Gardner's Manual on the Ultimate Rose*, we wouldn't smell a rose and think, "Am I smelling it right?" It is something like *not* trying to fall asleep at night, but by doing nothing, we fall asleep. It's a feeling as delicate as smoke.

3.

Luke Skywalker practices with the light saber but can't quite master the exercise. Obi Wan Kenobi covers Luke's eyes with a helmet, telling him not to trust his eyes, to use his feelings. For us, "Don't trust your eyes" means "don't watch how you are doing."

FOLLOW PHYSICAL FEELINGS

THE PROBLEM

Teachers tell performers not to censor, not to be judgmental, to take chances, etc., etc. And the performer goes nearly crazy trying not to judge, not to interfere, not to listen, etc., etc. But we can't stop ourselves from hearing, from feeling when something isn't right in the exercise.

And our eyes are on guard, watching for mistakes.

Actor: "Where should I put them? In a jar until later?"

Teacher: "When we look with our eye-socket eyes, we

are using our 'What will people think? Will I get it right?' eyes."

These eyes are saboteurs; they siphon off the energy that should be shared by the whole body and dissipate the creative impulse. But we can't turn off our intelligence when we act or do an exercise.

We have two sets of eyes — the eye-socket eyes and the eyes deep in the back of our heads. And we have two intelligences — our rational intelligence in the eye-socket eyes is helpful, it's the one that gets us to acting class on time. The intelligence which belongs to our inner eyes is the intuitive, wisdom-type intelligence. It is the intelligence we were born with and which hasn't been tampered with, perhaps because it's in a remote place. These inner eyes are benevolent, guiding us through the exercise, making us aware of what we are doing inside the body. They see, but they don't interfere. They see the invisible. They serve us without asking a price. They are our Awareness. They offer us Insight. These eyes may be too weak to see at first. They get stronger as we use them.

The How-To of Just Do It

Where do we put the mind that wants to jump into the exercise because there seems so much to correct? Of course we want to do the exercise better each time. But thinking, "I must breathe, soften my shoulders, I mustn't think..." is inhibiting. The mind can only handle one thought at a time.

- Start an exercise by breathing out using the F consonant. Don't think. Just breathe out. It is surprising how much falls into place when we start with the F breath.
- Find the right amount of pressure on the exhale. Finding the right weight of anything — of a

thought, of effort, of breath — can elude us for a while. We hit upon the right weight the way a kid fools around on the basketball court. The kid aims the ball at the basket and keeps at it until getting the ball in the basket is figured out by the body's intelligence.

- Make sure to feel the air passing over the bottom lip. That helps us to stay centered and keeps us from flashing on other thoughts. With our attention lightly on the exhale we are not tempted to use unnecessary muscles. That's a big dividend from a little technique.

- Take whatever thought passed through the mind while listening to a critique and condense it into a single word or a simple phrase. Let it stand for all the suggestions given in the critique. Don't think in sentences.

- After a while, stop using the F Consonant to breathe out. Just let the air flow in. It will know how.

≈≈≈

We may pace ourselves a little slower doing an exercise so that we don't feel as if we are off the bridge on a bungee jump. A slow pace doesn't mean allowing a gap in our rhythm. Use the 1, 2, 3 method, which was explained in the How To Learn chapter.

Sometimes our sophistication rears up during the lesson and interferes with these simple procedures because simplicity makes us feel stupid. A two-year-old absorbs enormous amounts of information and doesn't know from stupid.

≈≈≈

If simplicity makes us feel stupid, ambiguity can make us crazy: don't make something happen, let something happen, acting is thinking, act without thinking so much, care and don't care, have passion with detachment...And the ultimate in ambiguity: don't try...but don't try to not-try..."Ah," says Maxwell Smart, "the old Zen game."

7

THE ACTING CHAPTER

PART ONE

HELPFUL HINTS

The Warmup

When performers warm up too seriously it grinds anxiety into the body. Release muscle tightness lightly so that thoughts and emotions will have an easy transport out of the body to be shared with an audience.

The Audition

Acting truthfully doesn't need a long preparation. Involvement in the scene happens as swiftly as the breath swirls with the thought through the torso. Lily Tomlin changes characters instantaneously and is never superficial.

≈≈≈

Giving our name at the audition with that extra, extra brightness — "Hi!! my name is . . . !" is too much. Learn to keep it calm and clear. Instead of a shallow chest breath, let the breath be soft, coming from the bottom of the ribs, before speaking. It's a grounding and it doesn't take any extra time although at first it seems to.

≈≈≈

The actor waited so long to read that he lost vitality. Placing the scene on the outermost circle of consciousness would keep him connected to the scene but not too involved in it before he had to perform. Performance energy can be summoned when it is needed; the scene is fresh in the mind, the connection has not been broken.

≈≈≈

At another time the actor was to audition before the camera with a speech from *Hamlet.* He was confused. Either he would pretend to be casual and then have to jump cold into the scene, or he would be wrapped up in the character too soon. It helped to "half be Hamlet" as he waited to move to his mark. He was ready to perform when he got there. Staying lightly in character before beginning has other rewards. The producers don't notice the actor is trying hard. It is none of their business.

≈≈≈

Standing on his mark for what seemed endless minutes before they were ready to shoot, it helped the actor to feel his breath and be aware of its movement. He didn't find himself drifting out of the moment and losing his center.

≈≈≈

If a technique is not yet mastered, don't try to perfect it at the audition. Becoming self-conscious because we want to act the right way is just as bad as being self-conscious acting the old wrong way. Listen to what the other performer says, hear it, and reply. Doing just that much, you'll be doing a good acting job.

≈≈≈

We may audition brilliantly and still not get the part. That's not our problem. That's Their problem. We don't try to figure Them out. We do our work. Like the master chef, only if inspiration moves us that day do we do something different to the soup.

Once in performance, don't try to figure out what the public wants. The maitre d' worries about the customers. The cook stays with the food. Our job is to stay with the script.

REHEARSAL

THE FIRST READING

Some performers read so intimately they can barely be heard. Others bull through. Neither way is right. We don't hold back emotion if it wants out. Nor do we force a reading if we don't feel the emotion. Embarrassment comes when performers feel they must show how good they are. Not necessary. Read to make sense, trust in the words. Words involve us in the script intellectually and emotionally. We can't guess what the director wants. When we're told, we'll know.

≈≈≈

Before beginning the day's rehearsal, check the neck and shoulders. Don't press down inside the neck. If the shoulders are hunched forward, tense and protective, let them settle down. When we are busy we don't notice how uncomfortable we are. Settling down doesn't mean using meager energy. It means that we are using unforced energy. Feel an open space between the shoulders. This is where we work from. We don't act with the shoulders. Don't worry if some tension remains. Thinking about emptying is enough in the beginning.

≈≈≈

Sign on the door of a rehearsal room:
LEAVE YOUR PROBLEMS AT THE DOOR.
There will always be problems

≈≈≈

At the audition, the actress was being bold and showing a lot of energy. She laughed and chuckled, ran her hands through her hair and rubbed her nose, all with zest — and it was all phony. She was acting her cliché.

Having been cast, the actress was nervous at the first rehearsal. She lost her boldness, her voice became thin and her speech was prissy and affectedly upper class. "Love me," she was telling the others, "or at least like me a little, see how much I care."

We have to develop a feedback system which tells us instantly when we are sitting with our paws in the begging position.

The Nose

Notice how often people touch and scratch their noses. The habit is so strong that I've seen performers rub their noses impulsively in the middle of a scene. It's one thing to need to blow one's nose, another to grab at it because the nerve endings are screaming for attention. Try *not* touching and see how hard that is. When Michael Jackson, toured Africa, he offended the Africans because he repeatedly touched his nose. They thought he didn't like the way they smelled. The star's staff hurried to explain that touching his nose was a nervous twitch.

WORKING WITH A DIRECTOR

I suggested that the actress in a scene uncross her legs because it was out of character; she complied. But she also immediately sat up very straight: "Now I'm acting." Taking the director's suggestion is not the same as following a military command.

≈≈≈

When a director asks for energy a performer often responds with "extra" energy. All we need do is pay attention to what we are doing, saying, thinking. That's what energy is.

≈≈≈

If we rush to our part, isolating our scenes from the others, we will feel alone and without support and will experience generalized fear. We have to study all the lines that lead up to ours. Lines are connected in meaning and rhythm. Each part is embedded in the text and texture of the script. The whole text is a webbing of support. Anthony Hopkins immerses himself in the whole script when he prepares a role.

≈≈≈

PART TWO

28 LITTLE ESSAYS ABOUT ACTING

1.

Acting is a paradox. We have to be who we are — we have to be different from who we are. We have always to be who we are while not being who we are. Using the breath when we act is being who we are. We use our Performing Skills to become other than who we are.

2.

"That you were acting, not being" was considered untruthful acting by the Actors Studio, reported an article in *Vanity Fair*. This was the most serious criticism a performer could receive.

"Being" is in the infrastructure — the breath, tongue, nerve fibers. The breath brings acting into our being. "Behaving" belongs to the facade which includes characterization, motivation, the play's theme . . . all the accepted language of acting. By no means do I use the word facade to stand for something phony. The facade is important. But it is literary and abstract until it has become one with the infrastructure, the body and breath receiving the ideas. This is acting from within. This is what Marlon Brando would call "experiencing" the emotion.

3.

Two Bodies

Imagine that we have two bodies, inner and outer. I place one hand inside the other. The outer hand moves *only* because it is gently prompted by the inner hand. This is similar to the way the breath moves inside the body. It is the breath moving behind the eyes that prompts the eyes to smile, the mouth to talk, the hand to point, the brow to wrinkle. This is acting that starts on the inside and shows up on the outside. The breath sweeps out cliché and we act with what is left; our real response no longer hidden under the cliché.

4.

BEING OTHER THAN WHO WE ARE

We have to pass the character through our essence if it is to have truth and validity. But we must observe the truth of the character as well. In a production of *The Crucible*, an actor playing the role of a sensitive, poetic, Harvard-educated man in the seventeenth century spoke in the contemporary Chicago speech that was natural to him. He understood the role, and felt the emotion, but trusting his feelings for the part was not enough. We have to be careful that we don't try to be "who we are" so hard that we cheat the character.

5.

ACTING WITH IMAGES

Responding to an image and using a symbol as the final flash of intuition into character:

Meryl Streep talked about the character of Helen from the movie *Ironweed*. She used the treble clef of the musical staff as a symbol of the fading wino who dies alone in a hotel room. Streep's body was so emaciated in this role that one could almost see the treble clef in the curve of her spine. What the mind conceives, the body reveals. If an image occurs to us when we do a part, we use it. These are heaven sent. We can't lie in wait for them. But we can, with practice, gain access to our most fleeting images. An image comes to us intuitively. Perhaps after much thinking. Perhaps in a sudden insight.

To release tension in my tongue, for example, I imagine a feather floating in space; I feel my tongue moving lightly. For a cruel character I imagine a shark; I feel my lips curl into a predatory smile.

When we first use images they have to be correct; they have to serve the scene and the character. When we are experienced, the image can stand for anything.

I was in a futuristic play once in which the husband and wife were watching wide-screen television and getting their jollies from a program on cats mating. Not being a cat person, I went to the bookstore and did my artistic homework. I looked at pictures of cats, I read about them, I knew all about their mating habits, I got to rehearsal full to the brim with my research and my imagery and nothing worked. Not a tittle. Nothing worked through a goodly number of rehearsals until one day I gave up all my conscientious imaging and put an imaginary ping pong ball on an imaginary screen, the kind that bounces around while the audience sings the words. That worked. Go figure.

Symbols and images are private and irrational. They lead us through a subterranean corridor into character and the meaning and style of the script. Because a symbol is not so close to the action, it does not cramp emotion. It works because it keeps us from being too literal in our analysis.

Images that are as natural to us as dreaming may get suppressed when we act. That's as bad for acting as not dreaming would be for our psyches, I suppose.

The imagination, awakened by the breath, will supply us with a proliferation of images and emotions. The conscious mind is not quick enough to cope with the subtleties of a many-layered thought. Only the feather-light breath, in sync with our intention, can deal with such complexity and deal with it simply. How is the imagination stimulated if we do nothing? I don't know. What I have experienced is that I have a flow of images when I breathe and none when I hold my breath.

An actor asks: "Does the image come as we breathe out or as we breathe in?" There is no formula. Codifying the explanation kills it. Let images happen. Feel free to let go of one and something deeper and truer may come in its place.

Sometimes ideas float around in the imagination in no particular sequence. Don't inhibit ideas or be distracted by them just because they are out of order. Like a flock of birds, we let them find a branch and settle there until we are ready for them. An image can pop into the mind from any source: from saying the words, from poetic reveries, from vowels and consonants.

Images: Don't suppress them.
Don't try to have them.

6.

FLOATING AN IMAGE ONTO THE BREATH

The point of studying how to breathe in the first lessons is to become so familiar with breathing that floating a thought or an image onto the breath stream is a natural next step.

It took some time for the actor to get his first feeling of breath moving through his body. He kept a cynical eye out: "Exactly how is this breathing business going to get me a call-back?" But one day he really knew how to breathe out. He felt air coming into his lungs without helping it do so. And he liked being able to do it. Our first victory. For a so-phisticated actor, this was no small feat. However, he couldn't get beyond his acceptance of the breath. He didn't believe that thinking a thought or letting an image float onto the breath stream is all we need for the acting to begin. It is effortless acting. To the uninitiated, this is the last fin-ger of a precarious hold on reality to be twisted off. The fol-lowing exercise did the trick:

Blue Water

- Imagine clear moving water. Now, imagine adding blue drops to the water so that it be-comes blue moving water. The water is the breath. The blue drops are the thoughts.

We used a simple improvisation: a hotel desk clerk smirks at a guest who is signing the register. I explained that the thought of a smirk and whatever image occured to him would float onto his breath and as the breath moved through his body, he would feel like smirking; he would be-gin to act, to make-believe he was a desk clerk.

The Game Plan

Breathing out with the right weight to the breath and letting the air flow back in was the Game Plan. Nothing would change when he added character. The actor had to have the courage to trust the technique.

First try: He exhaled. Then he sniffed the air back in through his nose. That was blockage and he couldn't go on.

While he did the breathing as an exercise he didn't interfere with it. The minute "acting" was added he interfered, making sure to take the breath. He had abandoned the game plan.

Second try: He was determined to get it right. He exhaled Big. Gone was the subtlety of the just-right weight. Gone was the easy breath. Determination has nothing to do with the Game Plan. We cannot determine to be easy, to be simple.

Third try: He started, but his eyes showed worry. He was afraid if he did nothing, nothing would happen.

He was trying too hard. He did not trust the breath to do the acting for him.

Years of censoring, judging, interfering, and manipulating aren't going to evaporate in one or two tries. We had to wait until all the "stored up worry" responses were in the open and acknowledged.

I explained: "Really feel the air on the lower lip as you breathe out. This one small technique keeps out the flurry of needless thoughts, and will help you see the guest at the desk."

A week later, the actor's breath had a smirk in it. He had stayed with the game plan. He had finally allowed the process to take place without his conscious effort. It was actually easy. It was effortless acting. He felt natural doing it.

7.

OUR PERSONAL TIMING

Directors often don't give us time to process our images. They are concerned with keeping a scene lively. It's our responsibility, without scaring the director and while serving the needs of the scene, to manage to keep our personal pacing truthful — otherwise, the work will not be grounded and our timing will be slightly off. We need a discreet strength to withstand being pushed into reactions we know we do not want. ("Discreet strength" does not mean that we have to proclaim what great artists we are.)

8.

EXTERNALS

Let's not forget externals. Performers get unnecessarily distraught if, on the first day on the set, it is difficult to move around or the shoes with a new heel height are uncomfortable or the chair with arms feels funny. We make these adjustments fairly easily. Rehearsals are supposed to be developmental.

The external world is a wonderful place to be in, to get inspiration from, to trust. It's important to know what people wear, how they (both men and women) do their hair, what furniture they choose to have in their home. It's important to use a prop expertly. Setting the table with a tablecloth, for example. There's a right way of laying the cloth on the table and there is the rushed way, leaving the corners uneven because the performer is worried about the timing, about not finishing the activity at the same time as the dialogue ends. Rehearse as long as necessary to get the cloth placed on the table exactly as it was meant to be placed. Harrison Ford handles his props magnificently — from his professorial use of a piece of chalk to draw a diagram on the blackboard to the way he cracks that bullwhip when he's in one of those exotic countries.

But don't clutter up the acting. Don't let the prop take over the scene.

9.

Overcorrecting is a killer.
Self loathing is a waste of time.
Sentimentality?
Avoid it.

10.

GENERALIZED SWEETNESS

In local showcases and Equity-99 productions, I see many performers acting the same way:

with a smile

with a smile holding back tears

with a tone of intimacy.

The little hesitations, little smiles, little meaningless gestures are as studied as a Kabuki actor's. Everyone uses pauses and hesitations to break up sentences for no real reason. Fake acting. Mushy cauliflower. Those pauses and hesitations are interjected partly to sound real in a sometimes badly written script and partly as a private overture to the audience to win approval and to be well-liked. The performers want to act with emotional truth and honesty. But this work isn't honest; it has become mannered and ingratiating.

Language is missing. Language is the grounding of a performance, its strength, its confidence. Language connects the gut response to the material.

An actress: "We're told to forget about the words, to just find the feelings."

That is a big mistake. When we work only from psychologizing and naturalism we cannot discover what language can contribute to emotion and ideas. Without a feel for the construction of a paragraph or a sentence our acting is weak and we will jiggle our eyes and jerk our hands and manipulate emotions.

This is not boiled tofu to cure all ills. We may have the world's most perfectly placed elongated vowel but without an inner emotional life, we may as well pack it up and go home.

Writers keep asking us to return to language, but we aren't hearing them. We need language to help us strengthen the base of our performance. Michael Richards, describing the development of his character Kramer in *Seinfeld* says: "A lot of the little physical things are improvised...[but] It's my job to bring the character to the language."

OK. So how to do it? Work simply and directly. Do what's on the page. Say the words. Let the language, as good or lousy as it may be, play the scene. We must stop torturing the material by making more of it than is there and stop torturing ourselves by smiling and being ingratiating. Trust in the words — be present mentally and physically as you speak.

11.

I was coaching two performers in a scene that called for the woman to be sexy and attractive and the man, attentive and expectant. There was no reason why they should not have been able to play the scene. They had plenty of training and all their union cards. Yet something was wrong — they were not acting well.

The actress was beautiful but she didn't have the body language for sensuality or seduction. Her muscles were unyielding. The inside of her mouth was . . . what shall I say? . . . square.

The inside of the mouth is like a cave, dark and mysterious. It is always changing shape to fit what we are doing at the moment. Think floating seaweed.

The tongue, inside the mouth, is a strange and complex muscle. We have many ways of interfering with the tongue's natural, ongoing movement. We can stiffen a tiny part of it, we can make it thinner than it really is, we can control it with the mind. In an improvisation, the actress flattened her vowels so that they narrowed the inside of her mouth and distorted the shape of her tongue. She meant to be insinuating, but all she could manage when she spoke was to pound the words. Her tension inhibited sinuous movement, which inhibited a sinuous quality.

How could she be sexy if her muscles weren't sexy? The problem with her acting was not characterization or understanding of text; it was her body working against her. Acting is a matter of muscles and imagination.

She was unaware that she held her breath, which was one of the reasons she was tense. She had no zest for the words. She was so used to her tension she couldn't imagine what its release would feel like. And she had never experienced vibrations except in her throat, where they are harmful.

Her partner had a different set of problems. He couldn't stay involved in the scene; his eyes darted outside the established frame and his emotional commitment was hollow. He had plenty of savvy. He had become accustomed to the terrible conditions under which he had to audition — less than a minute to read his scene and fifty guys waiting their turn. He would get up to read having figured out a way to put a different spin on the reading from the other actors. The producers, the casting agents, the writers are sitting around the table and the actor was trying to psych Them out — to give Them whatever it was They wanted. That's guessing, manipulating. That's not acting. It had nothing to do with acting. In his efforts to get the job he went for the punch line at any cost. And the cost was that he no longer meant what he said when he acted. He had no commitment to the text, no connection to himself. He didn't need to psychologize about his problem. He needed to bring his talent, floating around like some unhappy little Genie, back into his body.

By working on the infrastructure of his acting, we found an approach that was strong enough to divert his habit of pitching the material rather than acting the scene. He learned to feel the breath moving in his body. This helped to harness his wandering attention. He became aware of words touching the blade of his tongue. This created vibrations which, like a magnet, drew his mind back into his body. Being in sync with his breath was an automatic centering which reinforced his sense of self. It helped him approach the material more honestly. Simple stuff. He had the sophistication but had lost the basics. We need both but we need the basics more.

12.

BEING IN THE MOMENT

Every acting coach talks about being "in the moment."

It was August, the hiatus was over, auditions were about to begin, and the actor felt "out of it" and scared. When a performer is that unhappy, forcing a "good" attitude about acting, telling him to relax, be playful, and take chances is pointless.

He had lost his sense of self, his center. This was partly psychological, but it was also shallow breathing, high in his chest, which served his silent hysteria. His breath had fear and desire in it rather than pleasure and release. He and his breath weren't working together to play the part. Physical discomfort was one reason the actor could not get into the moment.

Some performers can get into a script by deeply examining character motivation. But this actor couldn't disentangle from his shadow thoughts.

To begin with, he had to find his natural breathing which would enable him to walk into a room and, under admittedly difficult circumstances, behave naturally. This is not easy. It takes practice.

He had to trust once again that feeling the words on the tongue would help to anchor straying thoughts.

When we write a word, each letter has a top and a bottom. It is the bottom of the word that lightly touches the surface or blade of the tongue; an actual physical connection is made of word to body. By physically feeling the words, we engage the words. The vibrations that result from that touching are strong enough to draw the mind into the script, the performer into the zone, "into the moment."

Connecting script to body in this way will help a performer inhabit and lock into the psychological world of the script when nothing else works.

Athletes play the game best when they work from muscle memory, when they respond to the touch of a ball on their fingertips. Feeling the breath move and the words on the tongue is the performers' equivalent of muscle memory.

13.

PAUL NEWMAN'S KIND OF ACTING

An idea seeps in and influences us like milk nourishes our bones. Acting happens in this simple and mysterious way. We need not work so hard on interpretation. But when we are young we don't trust ourselves.

I think that is what Paul Newman meant when he said that he was aware of having worked too hard to create a character in his early films. As he matured, his preparation for a role became simpler: his imagination was more fertile; he no longer had "to get down on his hands and knees and look under the rocks."

≈≈≈

Simplicity. Just do it.

In his scene from *Henry IV,* an actor was unable to address the king ("My Lord...") without inventing a subtext. He wasn't sufficiently accepting of himself, of the sound of his voice and his physical presence, to serve the moment. He tried different ways to get there. He spoke very softly, he became a devious character...whatever. What was called for was simple, neutral expression; no attitude other than directness.

14.

THE TURN-ON IS TO FIND THE KEY TO THE IMAGE, THE PHRASE, THE ANYTHING THAT WORKS...

The actress came for coaching during the shooting of a film. She felt insecure. We analyzed the scene and found the thoughts. After I pointed out a good line reading, she tried to memorize it. The following is an unbreakable rule: *Don't memorize the emotion.* Think the thoughts. Find the key that stirs the emotion.

FINDING THE KEY PHRASE

In Strindberg's play The Dance of Death, the Captain and his wife, Alice, are sitting in their living room in what seems to be a quiet domestic scene. Actually, they are seething with hate for one another. A cousin shows up. The couple manipulate him, each trying to gain an edge. Earlier, the wife has had a tiff with their maid, who then walked off the job. Now, all dressed up in her evening finery, the wife must go into the kitchen, put on a heavy butcher's apron, and make the dinner. Wearing the despised apron, but affecting a casual presence, she comes back into the living room where the husband is doing a snow job on the cousin. In the role of the wife, I needed something to help me enter the room. I remembered a visit to New York one year when I unknowingly and regrettably contacted a couple in the midst of a deadly domestic fight. They used me in the way the cousin was used in this play. Separately, they each complained about the tactics of the other. The wife, affecting boredom, said, "...and then he left flowers at my door. I threw them out. I couldn't care less." I knew that she cared very much. That sentence, "I couldn't care less," got me through the kitchen door into the living room. I was able to play the whole scene on that key phrase.

But in the next act I wasn't so lucky. I picked up a wrong attitude and never quite rose to passion at the end of the second act. In that act, the hatred between the Captain and Alice has gone so far that the Captain leaves home. When he comes back, it is to tell Alice that he wants a divorce. She responds by throwing her wedding ring at him. When he's gone, she plots revenge. She dances wildly around the table, her hair falling down; she has become a maenad: wild, passionate, sensual, fierce.

It troubled me for years until one day I figured out what had gone wrong. Sometime before I had started rehearsals for the play, I had gone to visit a friend in San Francisco and literally walked into a domestic tragedy. I entered just as the Other Woman was taking her leave. Despite the fact that my friend's husband was an alcoholic and the marriage had been a hell for both of them, she was in tears, beside herself, distraught, the enduring victim. I had made the mistake of using my friend's real-life, grief-stricken response to losing her husband. No, no, no. For the husband and wife in the Strindberg play, a divorce is another round in a marital fight that will never end. The wife throws the ring at the husband with relish. No victim, she. She is excited by the prospect of outgunning him. They are a couple out to wound, not to kill. Killing would end the fun. Feeling victimized at that moment was the wrong attitude.

FINDING THE KEY IMAGE

In doing research for his movie *Hombre*, Paul Newman arrived at an Indian reservation where he saw a man standing very still, arms crossed and one foot resting on the step of a storefront. When Newman left the reservation several hours later, he passed the man still standing in that same position—one foot up on a step and his arms crossed. That image became the key to Newman's character in the film.

15.

IMPROVISATION

An improvisation helps us tap into emotions that are not immediately accessible. An improvisation helps to move emotions from the outer to the inner layers of self. Avoid using words in an improvisation. Busy making up words, the performer writes the scene instead of exploring it. Using obvious words induces superficiality; using gibberish is not good because the rational mind intrudes as we reach out for unusual combinations of syllables. Use numbers instead, or a repeating syllable such as BLAH BLAH. These don't require thought, nor do they detract from the emotional exploration of the scene.

The best acting is, in the best sense, improvisatory. In performance, the fresh approach to the moment comes from following the breath.

≈≈≈

When our responses are all worked out ahead of time, the body may be a little stiff and the breath a little bit held because we are too prepared. Most of the character's behavior has been programmed into our reactions through hours of rehearsal; we are not in a wilderness. We don't need to plan our answer. Really hearing what is said, it is as though we take the information into the whole self—as if the skin all over the body hears. Our presence is strong in the scene and we have done nothing extra to make it so.

16.

The Laugh

Holding for the laugh is in its nature improvisational. No two laughs are alike, just as no two waves in the ocean are alike. Kids playing in the ocean have a natural response to the waves. Getting dunked every once in a while by a big one that no one saw coming is to be expected. There's a way of being playful in the water while expecting the next wave. There's that same way of staying with the dialogue, of paying attention to the action while the body is sort of feeling when the laugh is coming, feeling it crest, and then speaking the next line as the laugh is subsiding so that no gap or air bubble comes between the audience laughter and the dialogue.

17.

ABOUT DISCONNECTING

I was very nervous at one time in my acting life — even the sound of my own voice seemed to violate me. I had to study the role without making a sound. I wasn't thinking of performance. I couldn't. I was too nervous. I realized later that I was incorporating the meaning of the text into my breath and my thoughts. Now when I study a part I don't grab at it. I read it silently. When my mind no longer needs to stay wrapped in its cotton batting, when I'm a little bored, I begin to talk with a bit of sound, close to my lips. This keeps me connected to my thoughts and doesn't put me to the test of acting. I increase volume a little more each time I go through the script. By the first rehearsal I'm so practiced in staying with the thoughts that the volume won't disconnect me from myself.

≈≈≈

Acting may be kept close in to the body, intimate, or it may reverberate out to the world — it is never disconnected from thought and breath.

≈≈≈

We can't apply this gradual process to cold readings. For a cold reading, breathe and say the words. Don't be careful. Don't be afraid of making a mistake. Don't feel compelled to immediately supply emotion and meaning. If we remain neutral, the words, in and of themselves, will have an emotional effect on us, will guide us to meaning.

18.

WHAT TO DO WHEN...

I am handed a script. Does the director want me to characterize? To just read? To read big? To read small? Who am I supposed to be? It helps to think "I know who I am."

I am my breath.

I feel the words on the blade of my tongue.

I will say the words.

It is the word on my tongue that keeps me within the script until I get a feel for a deeper involvement. I'm connected and committed to what I'm reading. Being grounded in this way eliminates that terrible feeling of not being in charge of my work—of having others in charge who can't tell me what they want because they don't yet know.

19.

RUSHING TO GET THERE

The actress was getting ready for a performance. At our first coaching session, her nerves on end, she jumped into the script without breath, her tongue so tight that her words were immaculately pronounced and totally unreal. She had fallen into that trap because she was eager to get to the performance part, to be rehearsing. All the fancy stuff has to be put on hold until the breath is ready and the tongue is moving freely.

20.

What is Truthful?

In his monologue the actor felt joy. Starting the scene again, he pushed the joy into his eyes to make sure the feeling would be there. After this was pointed out, he held back the expression in his eyes in order not to fake it; he acted with such detachment that there was not even intelligence in the eyes. He didn't know the difference between faking facial expression and having real emotions showing up on his face. What is real, what is truthful? And how do we find it? By going into neutral. Neutral means working with a balanced weight of effort, nothing in excess, nothing preconceived. If the face is filled with preconceived expression, we are actually compressing the muscles for the effect. If we empty expression from the face with determination, it is another way of compressing. Either will keep out expression. Often it's more a matter of muscles than of being psychologically incorrect.

Lightness is the answer. The ebb and flow of thoughts and breath keep insistence out of the action. Remember the Bird in the fairy story. Free to fly and free to perch. But Lightness is hard to sustain. It grows heavy in us. When we feel heaviness taking over, we mustn't let it settle in. Don't take refuge in that kind of hard work.

Eyes that are neither deliberately empty nor full of determined expression can *receive* the thoughts and emotions that the breath brings up to them. Think of our physical selves as a shelter for all that subtle activity.

≈≈≈

The actress used an image to keep her throat muscles passive as she spoke. One day I noticed that her throat muscles were bulging more than ever. She was overusing the image. Sometimes we lose the harmonious balance between desire and doing. We begin trying just a bit harder than is appropriate. Paradise is ours for a moment, then we get kicked out again, and so it goes.

21.

No Tempo

An orchestra conductor explained that he wasn't locked into a preconceived tempo. "No Tempo" relates well to theater practice. For us, "No Tempo" means that having studied, analyzed, and rehearsed, we don't carry preconception or insistence with us into performance; we let the real minute-to-minute emotions of the scene take over. It means no grabbing at our big important entrance. George Burns said he didn't go on stage to wow them. He went on stage.

There's this joke about the guy going across the yard to his neighbor to complain about the dog barking. No Tempo would mean he just plain goes over — No Temper (ha–ha) — and explains his problem. But this guy was caught up in his Prepared Tempo and couldn't change. As soon as the door was opened, he punched his neighbor in the nose.

22.

NATURAL JOY

After hearing her teacher talk about natural joy, the actress thought she was supposed to have a joy that the audience could see, that would cause a director and a casting agent to exchange approving looks. It made her self-conscious and nervous, thinking that she didn't have that joyous energy.

Natural joy has nothing to do with convincing the audience or with being adorable. It means staying inside the body and working with techniques which create vibrations. It means the physical pleasure of releasing tension. It is this that moves out of the body, almost like an aura, and this is what the audience enjoys.

23.

MAKING LOVE — MAKING ACTING

It's basically the same process. In the beginning, we are somewhat outside of the experience. When we are no longer virgins, the experience leaves the mind and settles down into the body and the body remembers how it's done and is playful and confident and full of surprises. In acting, the mind is no longer thinking about what comes next. The tongue remembers what it is supposed to do and the gesture remembers to gesture and the words know where to land and we seem to believe it is all for real.

24.

INNER STRUCTURE

The term "reveal codes" appears in some word processing software. It's an interesting concept we can add to our backpack of useful analogies. Working at the computer, what we write shows up on a small screen. Nothing else is on the screen to distract the eye. But where does all the related information get stored? Inside somewhere. These codes are easily gotten at by touching a button. Like the computer, our inner life is structured and complex with many commands embedded inside somewhere. In these codes are stored the psychological profile of the character, a family history, all sorts of insightful acorns we squirrels have picked up and packed away for the time when they might be needed. In good acting, the face, like the computer screen, is free from extraneous expression, clear but not empty. When it is appropriate, the information in the codes floats up to the surface and is revealed in the face.

25.

BEING SEXY

An actress was working on a character, whom she thought should be soft, yielding, charming. We could see her embarrassment; she was flattening her vowels, flattening her eyes and walking heavily in her high-heeled shoes. Her concept of the role frightened her. Her mind was peering at her like a nosy neighbor, her critical inner voice saying that she wasn't attractive enough. She was plenty attractive. But she was jumping ahead into performance. Instead of thinking the thoughts and letting herself open up physically to the emotions bit-by-bit as we do in real life, she was working for the effects. When she threw her head back in surrender, giving in to her lover's caress, she played the Result, throwing her head back ecstatically *before* her body felt the sensations leading up to that moment. She was producing an effect to make an impression: how she would look with her hair tossed, how her dress would flow. *When these effects are disconnected from thoughts and when they jump ahead of some feeling in the body*, they make us self-conscious. The actress was imitating poses she had seen in high-fashion magazines. Manipulated by these magazine images, she, in turn, was manipulating the images she projected. The sexy image was in her mind but not in her body.

There is nothing wrong with having a woman toss her hair back or of a male loosening his tie, each with sexual intent, except when the image seduces the performer to become manipulative. Acting sexy, trying to be appealing, is bad acting. Nobody believes it, least of all the performer. Sexual excitement is a result of connected vibrations and what is in our background Codes.

26.

RATCHETING IT UP A NOTCH

An invisible button is pushed causing perfomers to go into "italics" when they are asked to introduce themselves or when someone is watching them.

In the thirties, the actress Aline MacMahon invited the Broadway costume designer Aline Bernstein to the movie set she was working on. At the end of the day she asked her guest, "What do you think of it all?"

Her guest replied, "The actors and actresses are handsome and beautiful. But as soon as the director says "Action" they lose their beauty. All except Gary Cooper."

≈≈≈

On the last run-through of a radio broadcast, the performers were rhythmic, their timing was good. Then it was air time. At the "Go" signal they lurched into the script. They had changed all the values in the one minute between rehearsal and performance.

≈≈≈

Taking a short break before a last run-through of a comedy, the actors grew serious; they behaved as if the play were hard. They were draping themselves in negative cloth. Not necessary. The serious look is partly superstition — "If I don't take joy in it, maybe I will be rewarded. I will have paid my dues."

27.

A SENSE OF SELF

For some, acting before an audience is a snap compared to doing an audition or being interviewed. In all cases, on the scale from 1 to 10, go for a 4 and a 7:

We never allow ourselves to go below a 4 in personal dignity and a sense of self. No matter how anyone treats us, from the producer to the gofer, we stay at 4.

Go for a 7 in perfomance. 7 will not fail us. 7 is competence, our right to be acting. Don't scorn competence. Don't strive for an 8 or 9. If 7 happens to take off into 8 . . . let it, into 9 . . . let it. If we make it to a 10 — bull's eye. If they give us both ears and the tail . . . we take them.

28.

WHAT TO DO WITH OUR HANDS

Some performers can't act unless they put their hands in their pockets. When it's well choreographed, it's a useful gesture. Man or woman, it gives an air of casualness, insouciance, raffishness, innocence. One actor, in a play about family memories, had to introduce each scene by recalling an incident from his youth. He stepped downstage center, put his hands in his pockets and spoke directly and simply to the audience. He established an intimacy. He was sensitive and appealing. He did it for every scene. The repetitions, unfortunately, diminished his performance. With his hands always in his pockets, he narrowed his physical frame, rounded his shoulders, and seemed to shrink into himself.

≈≈≈

So many performers automatically cover the face with their hands when they cry or are supposed to register shock — that is wasting the face.

Crossing the arms over the chest for no reason except to get them out of the way is a trap. Once they are there, the performer is in an invisible strait jacket.

Do performers think nobody sees that they are covering up a discomfort?

We should be able to stand in the middle of a room with no physical support, with our hands at our sides, and be emotionally and intellectually involved in the scene. Gesture if it's called for, if it feels right. Breaking at the wrist or at the elbow is a poor excuse for a gesture. Gesture wide and don't be afraid of it. Don't pull back. The hand is an extension of the brain. Gesture is integrated with thought. Gesture extends speech. It reveals feelings when there are no words. Integrate the mind, the breath, the gesture.

Learn to act without crutches. It is very hard to do and we have to just tough it out. We must work through it until we are comfortable standing in space simply. We own our physical space. It is our birthright. Clint Eastwood said he took a lot of acting lessons to learn to do nothing, to just stand there. It's never too soon to begin. For my grandson's debut as Captain Hook on his fourth birthday, his parents told him: "Face the audience, talk loud, and don't hold your penis."

PART THREE

THINKING ABOUT THE SCRIPT

Think of it this way. When we study a script we deposit a continuum of unexpressed thoughts to the feeling behind thought. And even to the feeling behind the feeling behind thought. The best performers immerse themselves in the script, and the deposits they make will surface as they come into rehearsals and performance.

> ANTHONY HOPKINS: I like to keep my mind in neutral when I'm working... [O]nce you've learned the part — and I try to learn the whole film as much as possible — you've got the whole recipe inside you so your mind can make unconscious decisions. Somebody asked me the other day, "What is the arc of the part?" And I had to say, "I don't know."... I think he'd had too much film school.

≈≈≈

Many American performers are unsure of themselves when they study a Shakespearean role; they feel like imposters. One actor overcame his embarrassment and inhibition by studying his monologue as he walked along the beach until he felt as comfortable with it, he said, as if he were wearing an old sweater. Initially, he did whatever research was needed and then, by immersing himself in the speech, he got below the surface of his discomfort.

Memorizing the lines, knowing them cold when we act, helps to establish a subterranean connection and an emotional continuum. The great performances are those that never break that connection.

It's not a clear-cut rule. There are scripts where pure immersion won't work without the research homework. When I worked on Beckett's *Footfalls*, I discussed my initial responses with a Beckett scholar. I spoke with a Jungian psychologist about the reference Beckett made to a Jung lecture. I studied the *Oxford English Dictionary* to know the English meaning of words that Beckett was using. Everything I did drew me, in tiny increments, closer to the meaning of his play. None of it could I have gotten just from immersing myself in the script.

ABIDING BY AND DEPARTING FROM THE RULES

In our earliest training, we are taught to see and hear every detail in our imagination, to set the scene meticulously. As we mature, this inquiry should get tucked in the back of the mind somewhere and become operative in a non-thinking way — the technique of using subtext should become so much a part of us that we do it without consciously applying the rules. But it's difficult at first. One has to live with the discomfort of not interpreting everything and yet know that certain words take a slightly special tone.

Non-thinking is in that first flow of breath when we have thoughts without words. That's where the acting starts.

Finding one's method of delving into a script is to take one step forward, one step sideways. Several years ago, an artist was asked by a student how he made his decisions. He answered, "After a life in art, I don't make choices." He didn't separate his thoughts from his intuition. He trusted his responses. He may work days, weeks on a project but he trusts his talent. I find that I don't "make choices" much anymore; I follow the breath, the feeling of the word on my tongue, the image that floats into my mind.

I am not saying that we don't need to study a script, God forbid. There are scripts that attempt to reveal subtle emotions, shaded and delicate human responses that are not easily articulated. But even with the most daunting material, we have to let natural competence come out of its hiding place and do as much as it knows how to do. We need not wait for a lifetime in art before we begin to trust intuition. Trusting intuition comes after we have struggled with the techniques of character analysis; after the rules have sunk down into the body out of sight and generally out of the conscious mind.

Teachers have to challenge young performers to ask "better questions" and to make more "interesting choices." But if we hang on to this training we get trapped into making sure we are asking the "best," the "smartest" questions. One part of the mind approaches the script with intelligence and curiosity. The other part of the mind, afraid the response is not deep or interesting enough, censors it. We lose simplicity and gain fear.

We don't have to inhibit our initial response and deliberately ask our questions for every part we play. We want to avoid thinking literally or running whole sentences through the mind when we approach a scene. In life, mostly we think in shortcuts — half words and sounds. It's a gasp, a sigh, an "oh" or a "gee" or, given *Hamlet*, its Shakespearean equivalent. A remembered emotion or a physical feeling that passes through the body finally moves us to speak the words of the script.

If we immediately question according to a formula, before the passion to know, before we feel the rhythms of the script, technical terms like "overview" may dry us up. Each performer has to find, from the myriad ways to approach a script, the right way for each particular script.

Character analysis is great. Over-analyzing can give us an acting block.

THOSE CONTRADICTIONS AGAIN

It's a worthy struggle. On the one hand, if we approach a fairly easy-to-understand script as though we know nothing, we inhibit our built-in know-how. On the other hand, when we have a hunch about the character, we need to support it with lines we can point to in the script. That's very important. On the third hand, there are times when looking at a script as though we know nothing can be refreshing and reinvigorating.

Don't tussle with the contradictions. Have confidence in simplicity. First pay attention to what's on the page. Don't worry about deeper meanings. After studying the script, deeper meanings occur to us. Read the script without comment, without imposing anything on it. Read until there is a glimmer of what it's saying. Allow thoughts to come into the mind that are not prejudiced in favor of any one part.

ABOUT STYLE

In our lives we have the small moments and large, the mundane and the poetic, perhaps in the course of one day. We don't live in just one style. Performers get used to naturalistic acting, and feel insecure and resist style when a totally new mode of acting is asked of them. It's understandable. We finally manage to act with honest motivations and responses and then are directed to throw it all out for a batch of emotions expressed in what seems to be the opposite manner than the one we have been 'taught. We have to let our defenses down and be brave.

There are naturalistic plays and dream plays. Beckett and Brecht. There is Shakespeare and the Greeks and farce and comedies of manners and absurdist theater and the theater of images. There is performance art and gay plays and lesbian plays and parody, and in movies there is *Blue Velvet* and Robert Altman and Cassavetes and *Star Trek*...And then there's a work that will be totally new, not yet created, and its style will have to be figured out as we go along.

Consider these questions regarding style:

Is the work a comedy? A farce? A tragedy? A sitcom?

What is the tone of the material? Is it naturalistic or bizarre; are these recognizable, everyday situations or are they outrageous or fantastic?

Are these Monty Python characters who walk strangely?

What pace does the author want for the piece? Is it an easy pacing? High speed? Is it something like the timing in a Bread and Puppet theater piece?

Are we supposed to get a foot stuck in the bucket going to the door? What clues has the author given us? Can we find them in the script?

≈≈≈

It is the body that embodies the style. It is the psyche that accepts it. The style may be imposed on us by the author and the director, but without the performer there are only lonely words on a page.

Graduate Student: "Do you want us to be real? Or do you want style?"

Teacher: "I want you to be real in the style."

USING PICTURES

Looking at photographs and paintings when we ruminate about character and setting is easy and pleasurable. Put the script on a back burner and settle down with a large stack of pictures. *Life* magazine is good. So are art books, landscape and animal books, the Sunday magazine section, the society page. Let turning the pages be meditative.

Is there anything in common between the picture and the character? Look at the details. I once had a student who brought to a lesson the photographs of six society women from some glamour magazine. She talked in depth and detail about their clothing, jewelry, makeup, the expression in the eyes, the mouths, even how they sucked in their cheeks. She was able to improvise situations for each of the women based on her examination of the photographs.

Play a game. Point to pictures: Which one describes the character? Which does not? Why not? Knowing what is *not* is as good as knowing what *is*. It sharpens perception. Look at room decor, at shacks along a river, at the Eiffel tower . . . In what very particular setting does the scene take place?

Choose a picture and use it to explain the style of the script. Sometimes the less literal the picture is, the more profoundly we may understand the style. Don't shy away from looking at abstract paintings. A picture can even help describe the quality of a sound.

An actor who needed a good idea for a neurotic character found his inspiration in a photograph of a landscape. In the middle distance of the landscape was a sturdy row of bushes, probably used to mark the property. The sky was filled with odd, almost geometric clouds. The actor imagined the hedge to be his steadying center. Influenced by those clouds, he let his eyes become neurotic, weird. He had physicalized the picture and used it to induce a psychological state. But there was nothing overt, no movement; the only movement was his breath and his imagination.

When the actor was at the audition, he waited his turn idly looking at that picture and others he had chosen that reminded him of the emotional content of the role. This kept him lightly connected to his monologue without wasting energy and doing all his acting offstage.

THINKING ABOUT THE MONOLOGUE

We need not attack a monologue by laying our talent on it so heavily that it doesn't have a chance to expand. The way an amaryllis from its very beginning contains it all — bulb, stem, bud, flower — so a simple first reading of a monologue contains what the piece will eventually be. Speaking the monologue gracefully and rhythmically, we understand what the piece is telling us about its meaning and emotion. The way the petals of the bud open into the flower, the reading will be a natural organic expanding into a performance. Trust the words. Trust the author.

8

ORAL READING —
THE OLD FASHIONED KIND

1.

Oral Reading, for the survival needs of today's performer, is considered an elitist technique. Essentially oral reading serves the arc of a sentence, its breadth, its sweep. It serves a complex thought. Is it needed? Not a lot.

We live in a far from elitist culture. There is a lowering of expectations all around us; the proportions of life and art are smaller. No movie palaces; we go to the movies in a smallish room in a shopping mall. Our scripts are simpler and more naturalistic and contemporary, intimate, less verbal. Dramatic structure has changed. There's not much of it.

Today's acting is top-heavy with naturalism. The performer hears it from the director and the casting agent: "Keep it natural, keep it low-keyed, less is more." Getting an acting job is so hard that after a while we begin to set our sights for the part with a few lines in a sitcom that, in a better world, in a world of thriving theatrical activity, we wouldn't even watch.

≈≈≈

Norman Mailer explained on the "Charlie Rose" TV show how much he loved and admired the performers in the Actors Studio and that was why he and other writers (Gore Vidal, Gay Talese, and Susan Sontag) were giving them a benefit reading of G. B. Shaw's *Don Juan in Hell*. He was asked why the writers were doing a reading rather than the performers. Mailer, giving voice to a common perception among American playwrights today, answered that writers have a feel for language that performers don't have. We performers should be able to do our own readings. It is a shame in front of the neighbors that we need writers to give a reading for us.

Performers take scene study classes and cold reading classes and rejection workshops. Body building is in. Yoga and aerobics and personal trainers are in. But speaking so easily that the slightest thought shows through in the dialogue? No, this is not considered, it is not in fashion. Acting in a sitcom asks little of performers with regard to language, so why be over-prepared? Why take a chance on sounding artificial? Am I talking about theater? TV? Feature films? I work with performers who look for jobs in all three.

Just be natural. Look like the role, sound ordinary, that's all we need to get the part. But wait a minute — ordinary the way Roseanne is ordinary is raising ordinary to a special category. She is an intelligent and funny actress, and her mastery in changing tactics, tempo, and volume is part of her great comedy instinct. And ordinary was not ordinary when David Caruso and Dennis Franz, as detectives on "NYPD Blue," did an ordinary day's work. Their affinity with their roles was such that their most hidden thoughts were revealed in a phrase or a look. They didn't need words. When they spoke, their inflections were subtle. Their work was fluid. These actors were giving great performances in the genre of television. Think of the startling change in David Caruso from a caring, sensitive guy to a tough son-of-a-bitch when he locked a door and suddenly changed tempo and tone. These actors had absorbed their technique like the gold leaf that settles into the food.

≈≈≈

When I was sixteen, we drama students studying oral reading practiced our poems and excerpts over and over. We boomlayed Vachel Lindsay's *The Congo* for power and we quoth the raven for a tone of veiled meaning. We could "boomlay" and "quoth" at the drop of a hat. And we learned to change pitch and use pause for emphasis and find tone color in our voices. We practiced so much that the learned techniques became second nature. Does one have to be young and trusting to study this way? Are we too sophisticated today to practice something over and over until we get it?

In a prepared reading, performers, with no idea of phrasing, read from word to word instead of idea to idea. The reading isn't enjoyable; it's relentlessly hard work. This is a dismal experience for the performer and for the director. It is especially frustrating for the teacher since no one wants to spend the time to learn how to read. When I mention oral reading their eyes take on an odd look, hard to describe, as though I have asked that person to step into a refrigerated storage room.

2.

For a reading a performer has to know where the steel beams of a story are and to allow for the twists and turns of a character's thoughts and still keep the narrative line clear. If it is a piece of considerable length, the performer has to know how to apply a dynamic to the story. A dynamic is a change in energy to reinvigorate one's self and at the same time to renew audience attention. Remember Muhammad Ali's remark, "He don't change his tactics and I just picked him off"? Any tone that is unchanging becomes a monotone. If all words are given the same duration, they will begin to sound monotonous.

ABOUT PUNCTUATION

If we observe the punctuation we needn't struggle with the material. We don't bear the total responsibility for the script; there is the author's help. The author uses punctuation to group thoughts together.

The playwright Edward Albee wrote in a Dramatist Guild magazine:

> There is an enormous difference in time between a comma, a semicolon, and a period, for example. A playwright notates very much the way a composer notates a score. Playwrights write lines that are loud, that are soft, that have rhythms, some slow, some make it rapid fire, italics introduce stresses where the playwright hears them and stage directions indicate pauses when the actors must fall silent.

Most authors take utmost pains to indicate how the emotions and the rhythms in the scene are to be expressed so that the performer will access them as they were intended. Respecting the author's notation doesn't stiffen a performer's response; rather, it makes for a certain freedom because there is that initial intelligence in the sentence, the author being the first to feel the emotion.

Periods tell us that a statement is ended. Commas indicate a pause and that there is more to come. The comma gives the performer a bit of time to allow for a breath, and it gives the listener a chance to absorb the information. Question marks indicate a suspense until an answer is given.

Trust the sentence — the logic of the sentence, the grammar; subject, verb, object. A performer following punctuation is helped enormously in interpretation.

Rehearsing the role of Winnie in Beckett's *Happy Days*, every little dot on the page helped me to understand what he was saying. I paused shorter and longer when the direction said short pause, long pause. I hurried on with Winnie's words when that was indicated. It worked. Beckett, the author, was acting the role on paper. When I followed his punctuation I arrived at the emotions he intended. Sometimes punctuation is characterization; it will give us a clue to meaning and emotion.

3.

Those who have the knack for the spoken word, who can cope with language that is structured, have an edge. They have acquired a strength that is palpable. They command attention in a way that a less well-trained performer cannot. There is something about being able to speak that draws audience attention to what one is saying; performer and listener are bound as if by a silver cord.

We do get tired of the junk scripts. Eventually, no matter how starved we are to work, the mind refuses them the way the body refuses Twinkies after we've stuffed ourselves with them. But when performers who finally make it and want to stretch their talent and can call the shots and are brave enough to try a script in which language matters, what happens? If they can't handle the language, we're all in trouble.

Having said all that, I have known performers, rare though they are, who have never changed their delivery or their peculiar sound and have never given a false performance, whose work is a gift to the audience.

And, far from rare, there are performers that I have coached who need reading techniques but are auditioning and acting without them. It has to do with training. It has to do with what one aspires to. From indifference we do not make art.

ORAL READING CONTINUED

A Case History

1.

RESUMÉ: HANDSOME, INTELLI-
GENT ACTOR, 26, year or two of training,
has manager, makes hit with casting directors.

He came to study with me because his manager was concerned about the sound of his voice. It didn't reflect his personality or his physique. The problem was mainly tension in the mouth which pitched his voice unnaturally high. He was patient as I pointed out the way he put pressure on the blade of the tongue, or flattened it in the back, or even managed to put tension in the hard palate which inhibited the free movement of the tongue. He didn't resist the lessons, fine-tuned as they were. In a few weeks his pitch settled down and there was more flow to his sentences. His mother could tell the difference when they spoke long distance.

Next we took on the problem of a gap between what he felt and how he expressed it. His words didn't reflect his emotions. They sounded dry and disembodied. Again, he didn't resist my critique because he had felt that emptiness during a recent audition. We decided that reading a short story aloud would help. He chose F. Scott Fitzgerald's "Babylon Revisited." Incidentally, there is no better way to get ideas about characterization than by reading the work of Fitzgerald, Faulkner, any of the great novelists.

2.

He didn't get over his inhibitions easily. His words were garbled. I could see by the tension in his chest and shoulders that he was working too hard. His chest was sunken and his breath was trapped. He kept glancing down the page hoping to get an idea of what lay ahead so that he wouldn't stumble. He knew how to release tension in the tongue in an exercise, but reading the story was hard; it caused him to revert to stiffness. Even if everything else was perfect, his physical tensions would inhibit him; stiffness in the tongue, the inside of the cheeks...If there is too much interference in the body, the body is going to block the thought.

And all else was not perfect. It was now necessary to talk about reading skills, of which he had none. Each of his sentences started on the same pitch, and the pauses between sentences were all the same length. He felt more comfortable sounding every word alike. He had to learn to feel comfortable with a variety of sounds and pitches but he distrusted technique and trusted only sentimentality, which he mistook for emotion. Being self-conscious when he read, he was overly careful with the pronunciation of certain words, as though acting meant he had to speak properly. Alongside his polite pronunciation, he also spoke as he habitually did, saying "jist" for "just," "ontchou" for "aren't you," "meerr" for "mirror." He didn't know how to slur, which, believe it or not, is an important part of speaking easily. His sentences didn't end with a period, they just drifted off, which made him sound weak.

His intelligence aside, he could hardly handle a few words strung together. Reading without the help of punctuation made him feel totally responsible for the results. This made him nervous, which he then tried to cover up. He was suspicious of change, afraid of not sounding natural, like everyone else. In his case, "everyone else" meant the other performers with whom he took a workshop.

Fear of oral reading skills is part of the contemporary cliché of an actor who can't act without putting his hands in his pockets and who begins his anger improvisation with: "I don't give a fuck, yeah...well...shit, fuck you."

3.

In daily life, performers speak with variety. When they act, however, they speak in a monotone. The monotone and the thin voice are what is unnatural and artificial. Monotone cannot sustain emotion. It's the *dynamic* of pitch and pause and resonance and inflection that ignites passion. When a performer temporarily misplaces natural intelligence and a sense of humor, the simplest reading becomes hard work.

The young actor already had a manager and considered himself a pro; it was hard for him to accept the many details he had to practice. The details were beginning to bug him.

We have to enjoy working on the details: pausing without dropping the thought, changing pitch, emphasizing without pounding. Good acting is in the details. Details don't keep us from the whole. They *become* the whole.

THE ART OF THE START

When he read the actor jumped ahead of his breath because he was nervous and eager. He plunged into the words. He did not start his reading from the flow of his breath. Trust the words. But the breath comes first. That first flow of air, the source of the deep, private, emotional response, belongs to the performer.

It's the first sentence that makes the difference. It sets the tone for the rest of the reading. That is the art of the start. If we don't start that sentence with the breath, in no time we will be reading on empty.

There is thought in the breath stream, and there is thought in the front of the mind. When the thought in the front of the mind jumps ahead of the thought in the breath stream, acting becomes "acting," something we make ourselves do.

4.

When I use the phrase "on empty," I am quoting from a great article by Howard Kohn called "The Art Of The Sprint" from the *L.A. Times Magazine.* Performers and athletes have much in common. Kohn is talking about six champion sprinters training for the 1988 Barcelona Olympics. They run one hundred meters in ten seconds. One of them may become the fastest runner in the world. They live by the rules of their coach, Tom Tellez. "Start slow, start slow," he tells them over and over. Revving up too quickly, Tellez explains, means spending too much of the race trying to resist an implacable fact of science — by the count of three they will be running on empty.

One hundred meters. Ten seconds.

A slow start would help the actor pace the reading so that he wouldn't show uncertainty about what was coming further down on the page. His starting breath would keep him calm, make the paragraph seem less difficult. His flubs wouldn't leap out of the flow so noticeably. I wanted to teach him how to rob the bank: a young bank robber knows where the money is; an experienced bank robber knows how to get away with it. I wanted to show him how to cheat when he read.

Important as it is for the breath to flow freely, the breath also has to lift as it flows out to the words. There is good breath and great breath just as there is good bread and great bread. It has to do with the sculpting of the breath into a fountain of air as it flows and crests under the hard palate. The breath flows out in an arc; it doesn't come straight out of the mouth. It's easy to show the difference, but it's difficult to describe. I recently watched a Ghanian dance master as he struggled to describe what it is like when a dancer hears the drums: "It...it sweets you," he said. "You don't even know it but it feels so good..." That's true about the breath when it lifts as it flows. It is enhancement.

5.

We examined the narrative; how the author was setting up the story and revealing the mood, line by line. Paying attention to the literary values, we would, at the same time, study phrasing: how certain words must be kept together because they represent a thought and how that phrase must have a personal meaning for the performer as well as serving the author's intention. The more we study the text, the more committed we are to it, the more passionately we become involved.

The actor was half in the lesson and half fighting it. He complained that the story was written all on one note. He couldn't tell that it was his rhythm that was the same for every thought—the same no matter how different the thoughts were. It would take many repetitions to dislodge his one rhythm. It's not the explanation of a technique that takes so long. It's the time the body takes to accept new ideas. How many tries does it take to become an expert? "It takes a thousand repetitions." I've heard that from golfers and ballroom dancers.

Kohn describes Coach Tellez catching the runner Floyd Heard overreacting to the gun by snapping his head back.

> ...and today Heard is working on that single flaw, over and over. Tellez calls for at least four practices a week...Speed is the emphasis at half the practices, technique at the other half. The former leaves the runners with their tongues hanging out, but the latter is far more exhausting. They work on their technique until their brains feel

> fried...In that brotherhood of the right-
> eous, select few, there was no one who won
> on sheer talent.

Practicing until their "tongues are hanging out" and "their brains feel fried"; that separates the champions from the merely talented.

The actor was constantly facing what he couldn't do. In a fit of pique, he protested that his quality was unique, that casting directors liked his interviews and asked him back for an audition. I had to tell him that "his quality" without technique was a fart in a windstorm. (I'm quoting Brecht here.)

> No one wins on sheer talent.

6.

The actor read the story aloud as if in performance. I detected sentimentality flowing over him. He explained that he was "colorizing" the material, giving it tone. In the industry, colorizing lays a meaningless wash of color over an original black-and-white film so that audiences will find it more acceptable. To colorize a film is to lose the subtle values embedded in the visual and psychological concept of the film. If colorizing is an offense to filmmakers, it is equally offensive in performance when it's used in place of real emotion. Colorizing does not ask for an emotional or intellectual or any kind of commitment. It is indulging in the easily recognizable feelings of a nice person. In his eagerness, the actor was performing before he had thoroughly studied the author's intention. Allowing himself unexplored emotions led to cliché and sentimentality. I told him to dry it out and not to be afraid to hold back the emotion. Finally giving in to the emotion, it will be strong and inevitable. I told him to honor the structure, to know in his bones what the author intended, to allow his reading and acting to grow from thought, analysis, breath, intuition, and not to take the first trolley that came along.

We were in trouble. He was performing and I was rejecting his work. Once again, Kohn's article speaks to our experience. Tellez is referring to Carl Lewis:

> Carl had a habit back then of really getting his knees up, which looked marvelous to fans and to sportswriters, and Carl was proud as can be. I had to tell him his knee-lift was a waste of energy and motion...Carl listened and went out and lowered his knees. Extra knee-lift doesn't do jack for you. You've got to swing your leg through.

The champion gets past his ego.

≈≈≈

The actor was an avid golfer. He had the patience of the "select few" to practice holding his club with the right pressure — like holding a baby bird. He played golf from his character and his integrity and his training — not from his "unique quality." Why did he think acting was different? Was acting the Big Easy, some sort of voodoo?

Acting is the rigorous training of mind and body. The joy of the art is to serve it with loving discipline.

9

I REMEMBER FEAR

1.

Laurence Olivier's fear was legendary. Mine went unabated for twelve years. I lost trust in my impulses. I had walked into a spider's web of fear. I never saw it until I was covered with it. Even when it was gone I was still brushing it off.

Fear can come upon us for any number of reasons. Mine was seeded by a notion of perfection. The actress who came to study with me suffered for a different reason. She was having a kind of acting nervous breakdown. She couldn't help crying during the lessons. She interrupted her monologue to ask if she was supposed to continue. She would change volume from soft to very loud, suddenly and for no reason. She had no center, nothing tangible to anchor her behavior. Her acting was disembodied and ephemeral. Working from only the facade leaves a performer with mental interference and uneasiness.

"What do directors want?" she said. "They want us to be vulnerable and passionate." Perhaps wanting so much to be cast and because she could access her talent easily, she had made herself so emotionally available that her honesty curled in on itself and she became professionally vulnerable and dishonest. Her talent could not be denied. But she had to learn to leave it alone, to stop showing it off like a favorite child who gets pushed up front so much that it hides when the guests come.

As for me, I knew I had to get over my fear or I would have to stop acting. Finding my natural talent again happened gradually. First, I had to stop wanting great performances every night. Studying singing and having my eagerness pointed out time after time, I began to feel the clarity and objectivity of technique taking the power out of the vague fears that had permeated my life. If I could do nothing else, I would say the words of the script and feel them on my tongue. Primitive survival tactics. That is something to believe in, believe me; that is a blessing.

What is this fear most of us are afflicted with at some time in our performing life? We lug this pack on our backs so long we forget what's in it.

At the deepest level we know that we can act, but at some other level we persist in thinking that we are not good enough. There are singers who have become so insecure in their singing they can't even hum.

Trying to win approval accounts for a good deal of the baggage. It was a jolt to my students to realize how much wanting approval governed their behavior. But we cannot win anyone's approval. It is given or it is withheld. It has nothing to do with what we want or need from another person. It has nothing to do with what we want or need from an audience. So don't bother to ask for it. Do the work.

The fear of repeating an exercise after having done it especially well takes up a good deal of room in the psychic backpack. Saying "Don't tell me what I did! I'll lose it," is a common way of trying to remain innocent, but it merely puts one's art in someone else's hands. Real innocence is trusting and accepting one's work as coming from a moment of inspiration. We can be objective, know what we accomplished, and still be spontaneous in our discoveries.

If we panic when doing an exercise a second time, imagine the fear of not being able to recapture a good performance. I'm told that Olivier gave a superb performance one matinee. When a friend came back and raved about it, he found Olivier immensely distressed. Olivier knew he had been especially good but he didn't know what he had done to achieve it and didn't know how he could repeat it. We can't act or live in dread, thinking, "I was wonderful last night. How can I go back and act again? I may not be as wonderful."

We can lose our fear of not being able to recapture a performance by trusting the breath and the tongue — strange as it may sound.

Here's How:

We have learned to accept the spontaneity of the breath. The breath is somewhat different each time we breathe but always serves our needs. That's the first level of trust.

We've practiced letting the tongue move freely even though we don't know exactly what it is going to do. That extends our trust in the body's training.

Accepting the spontaneity of breath and tongue *builds up a trust in the spontaneity of each performance.* The hardest thing in acting is to give up control. It is as hard as not needing approval. Maybe they are related.

Acting is thinking, breathing, and saying the words. It has nothing to do with duplicating, worrying about being "as good" or "not good enough." Ultimately, we must come to believe:

> "It is not my concern what the stage manager
> or the other performers
> or some tyrant
> or the boss
> or my friends might say...
> It is not my job to please. My job is to think the thoughts of my character and say the words. I can't help it if anyone, including my best friend, thinks I wasn't up to last night's performance. I serve the performance, not someone's opinion of me."

A performer is one part biological, one part social, one part aesthetic. The biological self makes sure to go to the bathroom before going on stage. That's easy. But the social self has a harder time. Serve the performance no matter what. That is the aesthetic self. Even those who suffer the most with shyness or the "what will people think" syndrome can be strong if it is to serve the performance.

The performer is all too often on the asking end. The psyche takes a beating. We find ways to live as well as we can and still be performers. Our emotional pendulums swing from softness, fear, desperate brightness to strong, practical and wondrous courage. Hard as it is, we must find the middle ground between defiance and servility. It's there somewhere. It's as important as finding the job. We don't victimize ourselves. We never go below a 4.

2.

In a class in musical theater, the teacher made his basic technique seem so difficult that we students trembled at the very thought of going up on the stage and trying it out. One actor was so tense that his knuckles showed white on his clenched hands. When the performers were mentally slavish the teacher finally admitted them to his affection. It was so effective a manipulation that I found myself wanting to please him. Performers are such easy targets. What permanent damage is done, I wonder? Is that what we need strength for? To withstand cruelty? Wouldn't it be better to use our strength to learn technique with confidence and self-respect instead of having to protect ourselves from those of our teachers who abuse their power?

≈≈≈

It takes two to tango. The performer is only too happy to be the favorite, to be included in the ego games, until — beware! — the favors are no longer bestowed.

GIVING UP

Mme. Irma, the madam in Jean Genet's *The Balcony*, makes an inspired speech at the end of an act describing the wonderful rooms in her brothel where a man can fill his secret need to be Pope, Penitent, President, or Judge, while one of Irma's girls works him over. It is a moment when the actress must take the stage and address the whole audience with panache, with sweep. I have seen French performers take center stage splendidly. American performers blanch at stepping through the fourth wall and suddenly becoming larger than life. Playing Mme. Irma, I blanched. The more I tried for size, the more I felt my psychic walls draw together. I wouldn't stop trying. But I finally admitted that the speech was inhibiting and that I might not get the scope and would have to do without it. It doesn't always follow that heaven opens up — in this instance it did. Having relinquished the goal, to my surprise, I found myself gradually taking on the size and it was exhilarating.

I don't think we ever get into a role unless we empty out, really let it alone. We need to recover from all the effort and anxiety we've laid on the part. It's going to emerge or it isn't. That's hard for a performer to accept. We use a philosophy of life, music, prayer, a shrink, a friend, crystals, common sense ... whatever it is each one of us needs to get ourselves to give up. It helps to give up — and then begin working again. Just as we have to let go of tension in a muscle, we have to let go of that overwhelming desire to be good, to make it big. We learn to give up what we must; then we build upon what's left. What's left can be good, it can even be art — but it, too, is no sure thing.

I finally understood that however long and hard I try:
my breath will or won't connect to the word,
my tongue will or won't move on its own,
my nervousness will or won't go away.

I can practice the techniques with tenacity and passion and they will—or they won't—work for me on a given day. Believing in that helps me to reduce eagerness, to lay aside fear, to give up. Building confidence, practicing trust starts with simplicity and the acknowledgement of small gains. The four-to-seven ratio helps. I can go my seven, my competence.

There are no guarantees. The hardest thing in acting is to accept that we can't control or capture a performance, that we must find ways to let a performance alone, to let it be the words and gestures, the physical expression of thoughts. Though there are necessarily many lessons to be learned in voice, speech, and body movement, acting is finally connecting our thoughts as the character to what we feel, say, and do.

SOMETHING IN THE WORLD MUST HAPPEN

"Giving up" and "It's not all up to me" are concepts that some of us will accept, others reject. We each, in our own fashion, have to work it out. It took acting in two different productions, several years apart, of Samuel Beckett's play *Happy Days* for me to realize, in one of those life-learns-from-art experiences, that some of what helps to sustain us comes from somewhere in the world outside of ourselves.

In the first act Winnie, buried up to her diddies in a mound of earth, has a bag filled with: her hairbrush, tooth-brush, nail file...all the things she needs to help her get through the day. As the day wears on, her survival techniques used up, at an impasse and terrified, she turns to the umbrella, which she has saved for the time when she would need it most. But she outsmarts herself. Having raised the umbrella, she cannot put it down. Her arms are lifted above her head and she cannot put them down. She realizes that she is helpless, that something outside of herself must take place for her to be able to put her arms down. After an agonizingly long wait "something in the world" does happen — spontaneous combustion. Her umbrella catches fire. She is galvanized into action and able to throw the umbrella to the ground.

WINDING UP

Winding back in time from the nineties to the sixties, I see the path of my recovery. The sixties were a reverberating change for all of us. No generational difference in that regard. I could hear the tumbrils rolling down the street just like in *The Tale of Two Cities*. My insecurities were exacerbated by my growing concerns with the techniques of the forties which my age group were taught but which I sensed were no longer working for me. They were valuable techniques, no question about that, but we had not been taught that we must use them with a light touch. We overspoke and overcorrected. We had lost abandon. I felt my head about to roll.

In the sixties it was all about abandon. We were to throw away our technique, history, family, bra, jock strap...We were to recreate ourselves. The new, non-verbal mode of the sixties was enticing and disturbing. I am not by nature a self-expresser — a performer concerned only with my own feelings. It is my nature to relate to a larger concept. I knew that I had overdosed on technique and that some change had to come into my acting life. But I didn't admire the new group style of performance. I was distinctly uncomfortable for something like ten years. I was ready to lop my head off myself.

I heard of the Alexander Technique. At my first lesson I told my teacher there was a thumb on the back of my tongue. I knew it was my thumb but I couldn't get it off. As I began to comprehend the technique, I recognized that same pressure in all parts of my body. Even the first attempts at releasing tension were calming and led to a clearing of the mind. Finally, I began to think of performance differently. I saw that technique at its best was a paradox: precise and spontaneous, ever-present and invisible. The Rowe-McLellan singing techniques, and the Alexander and Tai Chi disciplines were based upon a knowledge and principle older and wiser than anything I could pick up on my own. I intuited that I was building a system that served my sense of what good, honest acting should be. I was more than ever a student of technique, but I was not trapped in it nor was I controlling it. I had found a way of taking the intruder part of myself out of the technique. I no longer acted with only a part of my natural talent, and I felt more confidence and freedom in acting than I had ever allowed myself.

So this is what I teach — form, structure, a sense of self within that structure, spontaneity within restrictions, the anchoring of the imagination in the body.

10

FAME!!!!!!

1.

Who needs it?

There are some who say: Think positively. Think great, not good. I wonder — do we hold ourselves back because we do not passionately think about our name in lights?

John Gielgud, talking about his life and career, wondered whether his ambition and eagerness to see his name in lights when he was young, made it harder for him to achieve the fame which was eventually his.

If technique is strong in us, if we do not fear performance, if taking center stage is called for and we take it, if charisma comes from vibrations, isn't that enough to think about? (Along with finding an agent, or manager, or whatever is needed to get the work seen.)

Want success. Don't want it so much that it causes even the faintest tension trying to achieve it. There are attitudes that enhance performance and there are those that destroy it.

If we're looking for praise, if we need it, we won't ever get enough of it. So it is the same as if no one notices us at all. Art is just art. We can't ask it to do anything for us. Acting is just acting. We do it to do it. Feeling a sequence of sounds and movements, feeling an internal rhythm, being focused, mentally and physically centered, is perhaps, in the deepest sense, why we need to act.

WHAT PRICE GLORY?

Pay no price.

It is the proper ratio between doing one's work and wanting fame that matters. We negotiate a balance between the private time we spend practicing our technique and the time we need to take care of business.

The manager and the agent are there to get us an audition. We can't do our aerobics worrying about what they will say about how we look. We have to accept ourselves, body, soul, and imagination, along with our potential. Doing what we think they want isn't going to get us a successful career any more than not caring what they think. In the end, we will have lived a life spent caring about the opinions of people who may not be thinking all that much about us. Establish boundaries—this far and no further.

≈≈≈

Much in this book is about releasing the grab—whether it is a consonant or a career. But if we've gotten comfortable accepting a B+ in performance we need not accept that limit forever. It is not impossible to go beyond it. The scary part lies in the need to be sought after, in feeling obligated to always be "on". We fear being the angel on top of the Christmas tree as much as we fear becoming the little tin soldier melting away. *Stay with technique*, with process. That's our bird in the hand, our soaring eagle. The fame and celebration are the end result. We can allow the unseen thumb on our art place to lift away. If very good is 10, we have permission to be 11.

2.

What's left after a bad performance or a bad review? I admire tennis star Chris Evert's rational acceptance of a defeat by a player who was not considered to be a serious threat. Evert said that sometimes it happened that she just couldn't dig down deep enough in herself to play the game she needed to play that day. If it happens, if we run out of gas on the freeway, the only thing we can do is accept it—

that day. The value in the experience is that it pulls us back into shape, puts us back on the path. And it doesn't happen again for a long time.

Do we kill a part of ourselves — no kidding, just a tiny part — for blowing an audition or getting a bad review? Some performers are lavish in their despondency. They reject happiness until they can have it on their own terms

≈≈≈

Happiness has nothing to do with success or failure. Happiness is a habit. Like jogging. Those who jog get hooked. Being needlessly unhappy does not enhance our art. We have to learn to be happy without the endorphins that are released by applause. Taking pleasure in a small success is an acquired taste–but enjoyment has to begin somewhere.

SUMMING UP

Acting is the energy and focus of our lives and we have to burn away the dross of our lesser desires. This newly awakened consciousness of simplicity, of being present, of dealing with the role and nothing else — nothing peripheral, nothing protective — is a struggle. It is a frail awareness doing battle with an older habit, the desire to make it at any cost to the spirit, and for a moment that older habit is stronger. What a price we pay to learn to have an honest response to the material.

≈≈≈

If you've got talent — I'm talking about a lot of talent — and got up and said, "I don't wanna be a star," it's impossible. It's impossible for you not to be a star if the audience

wants you to be a star and it's impossible
for you to be one if they don't want you.
It's the audience. They're the answer...I
don't try to be a hit. I don't sweat. I walk
out there and take it easy. I find that if I
take it easy, the audience takes it easy. If I
sweat, they sweat. If we both sweat we
don't smell good...

        — George Burns...Who Else?

AFTERWORD

If one could locate the soul
It might be just under the dome of the mouth
where the breath crests to meet the words.

BASIC EXERCISES

Whatever you do will seem insignificant
You must do it anyway.
  —Mahatma Ghandi

Breathing
Speaking
Laughing and Crying
The Tongue
Changing Body Image
Being and Behaving
Negativity
Coordinating Techniques
Practicing

LET'S KEEP IT SIMPLE–
DON'T HOLD YOUR BREATH WHEN YOU ACT

1.

What you learn in the fundamental technique, you will use in the most complex scene work, so don't resist an exercise because it seems too simple or takes too long to learn. The beginning exercises are not just for beginners. The more sophisticated you become, the more you will rely on them.

The How-To of Breathing

Do the running as described in the BREATH chapter first. Otherwise you may get too mental about these very good suggestions. If you are too careful or humorless about achieving good results, try a mildly distracting action to accompany the breathing exercise. Working rhythmically helps. It shows how easy the exercise really is.

To describe what breathing is like in my body, I use the word "air" mostly when it is outside the body. I use the word "breath" when the air is inside the body.

The F Consonant

The basic exercise to encourage natural breathing starts with *breathing out on the F consonant.* Breathe out and don't take air in. The air will come back in by itself at its own pace. Trust that it will. Don't start with an inhale. That's too complicated. For the exercise, feel the breath touch the middle of the lower lip on the exhale each time. Starting with the F breath helps to release physical tension and anxiety. With practice, anyone can blow air over the lower lip on an F. Feeling the air on the lip keeps the mind occupied and in the body instead of jumping outside of the body to judge and censor. Once the mind starts judging, it surely will start penalizing.

Find the right weight to the exhale. Enjoy trial and error. Getting it wrong is not a sign of no-talent.

With the right weight on the F consonant, the air flows back into the body in a natural way. Less than the right weight causes a meager breath and a faint strain as it comes back into the torso. Don't start the exhalation from behind the lower lip. It won't be strong enough. Start it at the lip and *feel the air touch the lip.* Some performers will take two years before they take this simple suggestion seriously.

Always work from the first small step in an exercise. Don't be in a hurry to eliminate the first step. If breathing is new as a conscious experience for you, at first nothing much may happen when you exhale on the F consonant. The body may not know how to respond immediately.

After the exhale:

The lungs expand like a balloon when they fill with air. The *diaphragmatic muscle* (which inhabits the space between the ribs and the abdomen) settles down out of the way to make room for air to come in and fill the lungs. When air moves out of the lungs and less space is needed, the diaphragmatic muscle sort of draws in and upward.

Feel the breath as it flows back into the body. After the air enters the lungs, the torso feels large; it is filled with air circulating front and back. The breath shapes into a column as it moves up through the chest, the throat, through the mouth to the lips. At the lips the breath meets the word. As simple as it is, this is the beginning of speaking naturally, with the words connected to the breath. Most of us need to learn this last part: to let the breath move *through the mouth to the lips.* Don't let the breath stop somewhere in the torso or the throat.

The *lungs* want the air. The lungs use the nose and mouth to let air into the body. The nose, mouth, intercostals, the diaphragmatic muscle, the chest, abdomen, and pelvis, all move gently to help the lungs get what they want and need.

The lungs' hunger for air is what draws the air back into the body. The nostrils and mouth are openings that enable the lungs to access the air. Do not *take* air in. *Let* air come in through those openings. You don't say: "It's hot — open the window and take in some air." You say: "Open the window and let in some air." When you take air in through the nose deliberately, you are tempted to tighten the nostrils, which distorts the face ever so slightly. The lungs get very little of the air you are busy taking. Incidentally, using the nostrils becomes a way of showing emotion; it begins to be part of one's performance.

Air is deposited in the bottom part of the lungs. That is the fullest breath. If you try too hard to do what you've been taught, you will probably always take the fullest, deepest breath. But you don't always need the fullest breath. Don't confuse a smaller breath with a shallow one. A shallow breath is almost always grabbed at in somewhat of a panic. It lands high in the chest and induces the throat muscles to tighten.

The air flows in and out for full or smaller breaths. Always let the cycle of air be completed. Don't stop the breath in any part of the torso.

In the following dialogue a smaller breath is all that's needed.

> He: Really?
> She: Why, yes.
> He: When did it happen?
> She: Oh, sometime ago.

Once you bring breathing back into your performance, it will all happen by itself—emotions will make demands on speech and speech will take whatever air it needs to reflect the emotions. (When you're told that something will happen by itself, don't get uneasy. Everyone struggles with giving up control.) Have air in the body and don't sit on it. Let it move. Be sure that it moves out of the body. Don't be conscientious about breathing in and then forget to release the breath. Complete the cycle.

≈≈≈

This next is a very pleasant exercise to get the feel of breath connected to a syllable. Make up a melody. (I thought the one I made up was kind of nice. I found out later that it was from the *Peer Gynt Suite*.) Start the singing with the following syllables. The SH will automatically draw on the breath, so begin with it first.

(Breathe) Sha da da da
(Breathe Sha da da da
   (Breathe) Sha da da
   (Breathe) Sha da da
(Breathe) Sha da da da.

Next sing numbers:

One, two, three, four
One, two, three, four
   One, two, three
   One, two, three
One, two, three, four.

The breath comes all the way up to the One. If there are problems, if you find that you are not connecting the breath to the W sound in the word One, start the One with an SH in front of it.

Sing the exercise using *words* that begin with an S, Sh, or F consonant. (For example: She Sings Sad Songs.) This is the easiest way to draw the breath to the word.

Speak the words. Enjoy doing the exercise until the breath catches on and connects to your words all the time.

Connecting the breath to the consonants S, SH, and F, is easy because these can't be sounded without breath. Most of the other letters of the alphabet can be sounded without breath. So an extra awareness is needed to move the breath all the way up to the place where these letters originate. Work calmly. Take your time.

The Roof Of The Mouth

The roof of the mouth is shaped like a dome. That shape has everything to do with vibrations, with resonance. The breath lifts as it reaches the dome. Immediately after it crests, it touches the word. In time, you feel inside of you that the breath is a large and beautiful shape in motion. You can feel that all the emotion that has been deposited in the body has floated up on the breath to that dome-like space. When it crests, it influences the sentence to move out of the mouth in an arc. Sentences that are in straight lines seem to have twice as many words as those that move out in an arc.

2.

THE PLACEMENT AND PHYSICALITY OF WORDS

PLACEMENT

Correct placement helps to produce vibrations. The Rowe-Mclellan speech patterns show where vowels and consonants originate on the tongue and in the mouth. They are remarkable in their perception of the true nature of sounds and their placement. Following these patterns you gain the full use of a sound, *with the least amount of effort.*

THE PATTERNS

Notice that each of the vowels in the first pattern touches the blade of the tongue from one side across the tongue to the other side. Except for the UH vowel (as in mud). The UH vowel is most effective when it is touches the middle of the tongue.

The vowels in the first pattern are: EE, IH, EH, AA, UH, AH. (As in: see, sit, set, sat, mud, father.)

These must be in their exact order because the opening of the mouth changes a little differently for each vowel. For example, the first vowel EE, which has its place a bit away from the tip of the tongue, needs the least amount of openness. The last vowel, AH, which comes from just in front of the halfway mark of the face needs a slightly larger opening inside the mouth than any of the other vowels. Try shifting the AH to the EE place on the tongue and the EE to the AH place. It won't work. It feels wrong.

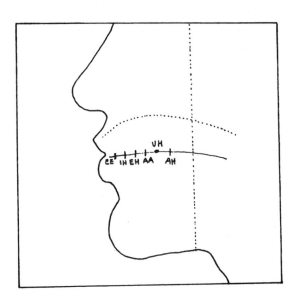

As the vowels progress from EE to AH, the space inside the mouth changes slightly with each vowel. Do nothing except feel the vowel changing that space and allow it to. This subtle difference is very important in performance because at the exact moment that you jump ahead of the vowel and open too widely preparing for it, you are anticipating and telegraphing the next beat in the scene. You lose honest emotion. It has become manipulation.

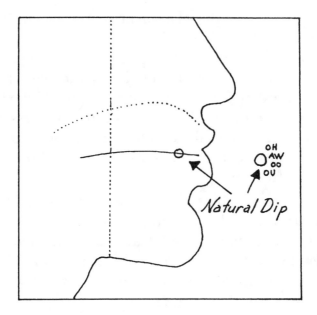

The vowels in the second pattern are: OH, AW, OO, OU. (As in: boat, bought, boot, could.)

These fall into the natural dip in the tongue. You can see or touch the natural dip with a finger. They are given in this order only to keep the exercise consistent.

The lip corners float UP for the vowels in the first pattern. They float FORWARD for the vowels in the second pattern. It makes a big difference in the sound when the lip corners move with the vowel. After you practice a while it will become automatic. *Float* up or forward. Don't muscle it.

A performer has to practice different shapes for the EE IH EH AA UH AH and OH AW OO OU vowels the same way an artist practices making a circle, an oval, an arc, a half circle. If you think of the vowel as having a *shape*, you will not feel that changing your speech habits will make you sound affected.*

---

*   In any speech book there is a Phonetics page listing vowels and consonants in their ideal shape.

When practicing the placement of vowels and consonants, start by being exact about the placement for each letter. Doing this in the beginning, helps to change habits.
Mentally see the place on the tongue for each vowel. Then
speak. The learning isn't finished until the mind is no longer
controlling the tongue. It's a back-and-forth process of trying to leave the tongue alone to do what it knows and then
use a sort of bio feedback that tells you to be a little careful
about your placement.

In time, you are able to recognize what feels right and *is*
right and what has to be corrected. At first, you may be placing the words properly but a bit too carefully. The teacher
says: "Work with more confidence, be more casual." You try
to be less concerned and thereupon lose the placement.
However, you quickly regain it.

All of the techniques call for detailed homework and no
amount of psychological understanding or concentration or
"private moment" is going to give it to you. You don't plant
potatoes by examining your true feelings about them. You
go to the basics: dig a hole, add water and potato nourisher
and whatever else one does to a potato.

In addition to keeping the words clear of the throat area,
you need placement to keep them from landing between the
cheek bone and the molars. This is a grey area where the
words sound sort of hollow. There is nothing in this part of
the mouth that serves volume or clarity or resonance. When
performers feel that a sound is hollow, they press on the
words, hoping to feel vibrations. But pressure stops vibrations.

For an exercise in bringing vowels and consonants to the
front half of the face, place your forefingers at the chin and
direct the syllables towards the fingernails. Or pretend you
are hanging the vowels out to dry like bedsheets on a
clothesline.

Physicality

There is a very slight change in lip and tongue movement in pronouncing each of the following consonants: V Z S TH (voiced and unvoiced) W WH Y F SH J H M N P B K G T L R. Especially make sure that L G K R land in the middle of the blade of the tongue, roughly where the EH vowel is spoken. These are the ones that are most often misplaced causing an unpleasant sound or, in the case of the R consonant, causing great tension in the sides of the tongue, which narrows the mouth's opening and inhibits its movement.

The consonants M V B, that originate at the lips, tend to slip back into the mouth. Don't let them. (Once the body feels the difference, this doesn't seem like esoteric information.)

Richness and variety are embedded in these consonants. Allow for their differences, however slight they may be. Play with these letters and discover exactly the place where each consonant is pronounced. Resist the temptation to overdo these differences. Awareness of the differences is almost all that's needed.

3.

The Art Of Laughing and Crying Using Techniques of Placement

Performers worry about being phony when a moment calls for laughter or tears. They think they have to be, literally, moved to laugh or cry. They are afraid that technique is fake. You're not always given God's gift of laughter and tears when you're acting. If you don't happen to respond spontaneously, it is perfectly valid to trust the physical changes in the body. It is actually more honest than straining to feel something. The following techniques help to start LAUGHTER:

The placement for the consonant H is in front of the halfway mark of the face, at the EH place on the tongue. The vowel AH is the last vowel of the first pattern. The placement of the H and the AH is very important. If the HAH lands on the back of the tongue it will stop the ongoing movement of the HAHAHA.

Begin by speaking the HAHAHA simply, as vowels, nothing more. Just feel its place on the tongue.

Next let the HAHAHA connect to a feeling of laughter. No need to force it. Don't press down in the body to generate sound. Pressing down keeps it from happening.

Laughter will begin. Let it grow. In your eagerness to be really laughing, don't throw away the vowel shape too soon.

Let laughter move into the eyes. It will. Don't try to force it. As the laughter becomes infectious, let it sound any which way.

When the laughter begins to wane, bring in the HA-HAHA vowel again. Working from the vowel is actually what keeps the laughing truthful, strange as it may seem.

Check the myriad places in the body that may tighten slightly. That slightest tension will cause embarrassment and make the laughter feel hollow. The body as well as the mind has to want the laughter and accept it when it comes.

For CRYING:

Short quick breaths and the H connected to the UH vowel or the UH vowel by itself can start the crying. The breaths and the vowel together with the thought of crying, brings a sadness into the eyes and real crying begins. I find it necessary to be specific in my directions in order to avoid a half-explained technique. Try these suggestions my way and then adapt them according to your own experience.

4.

RELEASING TENSION IN THE TONGUE

The Main Points

Let the tongue move. Don't make it move. The tongue doesn't move if:

> you press down on the blade
> or the back
> or curl the sides
> or tense the underneath part
> or watch over it.

Imagine a conveyor belt in the school cafeteria moving the dishes forward through the open window into the kitchen. When the belt is stopped, the dishes don't move. They pile up until they spill onto the floor. Think of the tongue as a conveyer belt for words. If the tongue doesn't move, the words pile up inside the mouth. On the vaudeville circuit, it was called the Mushmouth Routine.

Use the tongue to transport the words from inside the mouth to the outside world.

A tight tongue can be released by mental, thought-directed techniques:

Feel the back of your tongue floating up in the mouth.

Feel your tongue getting fatter. Feel it to be light, fluffy, happy. This may sound to some as if you are a little ditsy—but your tongue will be free. Who knows what condition theirs are in?

Feel the tongue's full size. The larger the surface, the more vibrations.

When I observe performers warming up their voices, I

hear a lot of forced sound. I see no one releasing tension in the facial muscles that inhibit sound.

Never mind projecting. Think the jaw-hinge loose, the upper lip and lip corners released from tension, the tongue full and moving. Let the inside of the cheeks be soft, moist, vulnerable — as innocent as a baby's. Don't expect releasing tension to need some large movement. It can be extremely small and still be effective.

The following are physical, less subtle, techniques:

For the tongue to feel full and larger, slip it out of the mouth and let it rest placidly on the lower lip, like a seal sitting contentedly in the sun. Tongues are self-conscious, they quiver when they have to leave that dark safe place in the mouth. Slip the tongue back into the mouth and let it stay full. Don't *make* it full.

The Pull of Gravity

With the knees spread, and the face towards the floor feel the pull of gravity, a buzz, coming from below. Wait to feel the buzz.

Then give in to it and descend towards the floor — but not all the way. Bend forward from the waist, not the neck. Leave the back of the neck alone. Don't curve it.

Don't thrust the chin forward. Be easy. Giving in means letting the buzz pull the tension out of your cheeks, lips, lip corners, and tongue. Sometimes the tongue will still feel like a piece of wood after all your efforts. Don't worry about it.

Don't work too slowly, trying to feel everything. Slowness lets in self-consciousness. Trust in the pace.

Gently come up and stay free in the face. Because tension is a habit, it will want to come back. Watch out for it. Gently avoid it.

Released from tension, the face may feel gross. It isn't.

The face is more beautiful when it is its true size instead of being pulled together by taut muscles. Give up control and discover new feelings. With each release, the body releases tension in unexpected places.

As you continue this exercise and get closer to a normal sitting position, it is tempting to tense the shoulders. Don't.

Repeat the exercise and speak the BLAH BLAH syllable as you float upwards. Using the BLAH BLAH syllable avoids the concern for getting the exercise right. Keep the BL at the lips. Don't let the AH fall back near the molars. Feel the BLAH touch and bounce off the blade of the tongue. Neither pound the tongue with the BLAH nor let the tongue grab at the BLAH to make sure it touches.

Don't press any syllable too hard on the tongue.

Don't think a thought too hard.

Don't breathe too "correctly."

Don't be eager.

Another way to loosen the tongue is to talk as though there were no muscle in the tongue. It will sound plenty dumb. Don't be put off. Speak a practice sentence. I've used this one for years: "The ship sailed into the Mediterranean. A world cruise, the passengers were very rich." It's helpful to use the same sentence because you get to know it well and can try out all your techniques on it — placement, freeing the tongue, improvisations, characterizations, etc. Be sure the words don't fall into the back part of the mouth. Keep them in front no matter how slack the tongue muscle is. When face and tongue are no longer being controlled, speak a little more clearly. Speaking a little more clearly doesn't require that you tighten the tongue in order to be understood. All you have to do is intend to speak more clearly and you will be clear.

Think the thought and *let* the tongue move. Even when

the tongue stays loose, the words will be clear. Don't control the tongue as if it might not say the words if you didn't control it. Take a chance. See what happens. (This is one of those maddening moments where, on the one hand, you're told to do a movement precisely and on the other, you're told not to be so careful.)

Sometimes performers learn more from my making a mistake than when I execute a technique perfectly. Being short of breath or unable to release the tension in my tongue on a given day is real, it happens, and it's helpful to see the teacher trying various techniques to get out of a tough spot. It's hard to say what to do about being nervous, about the breath that isn't available to you, no matter how willing you are to be available to it. Sometimes all you can do is accept that today the breath is elusive and the tongue stiff. Often just that awareness is calming and you may begin to work more easily.

The upper lip can be quite tense without your noticing it. It does not give strong signals of tension the way the back of the neck or the shoulders do. It distorts the face. It creates resistance to the flow of speech.

To release tension in the upper lip:

Like a summer's breeze moving an awning, blow air softly under the lips. That is the only physical movement. Everything else is the desire to have the lip feel free. When the upper lip is really relaxed there is a slight flutter of the lips as the air blows through them. Don't try to achieve the flutter by pressing hard on the lip corners. Don't become more involved with the flutter than with freeing the lips. That is being Result Oriented, jumping ahead to win the prize. Allowing Process lets one action follow another; it keeps the psyche with the action. If you can learn to trust in the Process in a simple exercise, you will, in performance, not anticipate a question or worry about the response.

VOLUME

You're told to speak louder and your first impulse is to tighten the muscles to make a bigger sound. On paper this is clearly illogical. But, with a production under way and much at stake, you lose logic and go for the grab.

Have the intention to be louder; intention without tension.

Let the words draw on more breath. The words will know how much breath they need to support the greater volume.

The vibrations from the blade of the tongue will add volume.

Don't lose placement.

Don't let added volume separate thought from words. First think the sentence with its meaning. Then keep the sentence close to the lips and whisper it. Allow for more volume each time you repeat the sentence. Keep connected to the thought.

5.

A BEGINNING RITUAL — THE SEQUENCE

Most artists and athletes have a beginning ritual. I begin with what I call a sequence: I breathe out on the F consonant, letting the air flow back in to my body. I do this three times. When I feel the breath moving, I try out the BLAH sound. If that feels comfortable, I let my tongue play with several BLAH sounds the way a child plays: BLAH BLAH BLAH BLAH.

To coordinate breathing with speaking, I practice the sentence: (Breathe) THE SHIP SAILED INTO THE MEDITERRANEAN, A WORLD CRUISE, THE

PASSENGERS WERE VERY RICH. First I think the thoughts and use the BLAH BLAH in the place of words. When I feel that I am making free sounds I try the words. I breathe at the commas. By the time I have finished this sequence of breath to the BLAH to a freely moving tongue to the words of my practice sentence, I am ready to work with my script.

6.

THE BODY

Before working on body changes for a character examine your body as you experience it habitually.

The actor had a revelation when he realized that growing up he had put great physical pressure into his body in order to repress his emotions.

> Know thyself
> —Socrates

That includes psyche and soma.

You can feel a place that is tight. Breathe out on an F. Think the word *soft*. Or the word *empty*. Or think whatever you want. Direct a thought to that place with whatever image of emptiness occurs to you. Whatever it is that you do to release tension, do it. Don't continue to act with tension. Take the time to figure out how to correct the problem.

Discover what part of the body tightens when acting begins. Do you press down at the lip corners? Do you raise the shoulders and bring them forward? Does your big toe stiffen? Do you, ever so slightly, squeeze the muscles at the corners of the eye?

Bring the attention to that place and empty it while breathing softly.

Bring sound into the body while keeping that place empty. Avoid text. Use the BLAH BLAH.

Speak a word keeping that place empty. The only way to remove tension is to work in small increments.

Think your dialogue without emotion. Then add emotion. If emotion brings the tension back, you are not ready to work on the script. Don't let yourself get away with anything. Be patient.

When the time comes, Act. (Hear, respond and mean what you say.)

When it's over, put on the Lab Coat.

7.

USING PICTURES

Using pictures helps you to examine and change body behavior. Peruse a large stack of photographs and reproductions of paintings.

Which body shape in the picture fits your body image? Which body shape is the ideal? Pointing to a picture helps to objectify your thoughts and this helps you to understand yourself more clearly.

Which photos show a body shape with tension? Without tension? Examine the picture closely. Look at the thumb, the big toe, the cord in the neck...

Relate this to your personal tension.

Choose those pictures that fit your body image while also being ideal, confident body shapes. Study the true shape of the whole physique, the muscles, the positioning of the feet, the hands, etc.

8.

THE FOUR POINTS

You want to lower your emotions and thoughts to get below that part of the mind that talks too much and tries too hard. I put my hand below my eyes indicating that the work take place from there on down. It helps. If you breathe too high, if you think too high, a tension sets in the body. Lower the learning, lower the acting, lower the breath.

When the attention is lightly on what I call the four points, the shoulders and hips, it keeps thoughts from bunching up in the mind. The actress in front of the camera knotted her forehead too much. Directing her attention down to the four points, she was able to keep her intensity by supporting it with the body as well as the mind. Her forehead didn't have to carry the full burden of expression. When you have the support of the body you are less tempted to freak out courtesy of self-criticism. The mind cannot take the whole burden of the acting because it is not equipped to do it all. When it does, it does part of the acting and then it worries. Worrying takes the energy away from the task, leaving you about 10 percent of your talent with which to act.

9.

NEGATIVITY — WRITING IT OUT

You have to be aware of and acknowledge how you feel, really feel, about what you are doing. No bullshit. Bring your hidden attitudes to the surface. It helps, when coping with negativity, to pour thoughts out on paper, writing in a stream of consciousness until you have figured out what is bothering you. All thoughts are human — some are shameful, but human nonetheless. You have to face your weaknesses and, however infinitesimal, your strengths. Don't try to write well; if you feel dumb, write dumb. The important thing is to uncover whatever is cluttering the mind. So that there is no temptation to write cleverly, tear up the pages when there's no more to say, when you have exhausted your ramblings. Fighting hard to keep from feeling negative sometimes sets you back for a longer time than if you admit to it, write it out, and let it settle down.

10.

BEFORE THE REHEARSAL

The following is your private preparation before any rehearsal begins. Let us say that your first speech opens the act.

> CHARACTER: We were a big family. And all of us
> lived at home.

Work technically—that is, work with proper placement, with breath and a freely moving tongue. Breathe the F breath out. Feel the breath move back into the body. It has to. It is involuntary. Don't let it get stuck in the torso somewhere. The breath floats all the way up to the lips. Play around with the vowels and consonants in the first sentence to remind the tongue where the vowels belong. Something like this:

For the word "we" in the first sentence, connect the "w" to each vowel: (lip corners floating up) WEE, WIH, WEH, WAA, WUH (as in mud), WAH, and (lip corners floating forward) WOH, WAW, WOO, WOU (as in could).

For the words "we were," connect the two words to each vowel: WEEWEREE, WEEWERIH, WEEWEREH, etc.

This gets the tongue moving and at the same time the vowels are continually touching their marks on the tongue.

For the words "we were a big": WEEWERABEE, WEEWERABIH, etc. Notice that I am connecting the words by their consonants.

For the words "big family" connect the G to the F, like this: GFEE, GFIH, GFEH, GFAA, etc.

And so on with the words in the next sentence. By the end of this drill, you have practiced placement and the tongue remembers what to do in natural and spontaneous action.

Feel the tongue full and without tension. If you are nervous, and the tongue is still tight, use the BLAH BLAH syllable. These exercises are for the release of tension so that you can be entirely comfortable when finally you turn your dialogue over to the words. When it feels like a free sound, a positive feeling, speak. Another good substitute for words is numbers. For example: the sentence "We were a big family" has seven syllables. Actually use numbers one through seven to speak the sentence. Using words too soon inhibits the breath and tightens the tongue — the body remembers the wrong way for a long time before it gives up. Using as many numbers as there are words in the sentence and matching the syllables in a word with the correct amount of numbers maintains the rhythm and emotion of the sentence.

You are teaching the body not to bring tension along with emotion. When the sound of your voice is non-threatening to you, try speaking words. If it feels good include walking. Just walk. Don't try to walk a "correct" way. Walking has a way of neutralizing nervousness. When you feel able to breathe and walk (I don't mean to be funny; many people hold their breath when they walk), add BLAH BLAH to the walking. Start the scene using BLAH BLAH for the first line of dialogue. Then use numbers. Discard the BLAH BLAH and the numbers when you feel calm. Speak the words. Work with a light heart. Think of blowing soap bubbles.

Follow instructions as best you can, but don't worry about the preparation being exactly right. More or less, right now, is better than being too careful.

In addition to the thought you have already given to the script, this drill is a way to work on your role subliminally.

BEING AND BEHAVING BECOMING INSEPARABLE

These are exercises for the body when work on the script begins. BEING refers to the infrastructure: the breath, the mouth, tongue, lips, the torso, ribs, legs, arms, etc., all of which, you now deeply identify with acting. BEHAVING is working with the script in hand. It includes play analysis, character analysis, style . . . all the work the author has done on the manuscript.

Begin to study the part sitting down. Sitting is less complicated than standing.

Advance to standing but lean with the spine against the wall for support. Think the character's thoughts using the BLAH BLAH in place of words. When you feel ready, think the thoughts and say the words of the script.

Stand in the middle of the room with no support. But keep your hands behind your back to remind yourself that you are not yet fully acting. Think your thoughts and say the words.

Finally, be able to stand in a space with no support and feel totally involved in the scene with your hands confidently at your side, and act. Gesture if you feel moved to it. Accept your psyche as well as your shoulders, hips, arms, legs, and hands. You are ready for rehearsal, you have removed self-consciousness, you can hear what the director is saying instead of hearing only your self-criticism.

≈≈≈

You are at a first blocking rehearsal. The director says: "Standing at the side of the stage, begin the play by sharing your memories with the audience. It's a mood piece."

Breathe. The breath moving through the body is going to touch the imagination and something about the play or the character will come into your mind. Trust it. Then say the words. Don't be guarded. After that placement review, you are tuned up. Turn the words over to the tongue. Your talent is in your tongue. Let it say the words. Even if you had no hint other than the description and the immediate dialogue, saying the words with a freely moving tongue would generate character to some extent. This is as good a way to begin as any.

11.

PRACTICING

It's not easy to start your exercises. There comes that moment when you make a decision to practice. It is a decision. Once that is made you have to create a moat around you of quiet, of readiness. There must be nothing else in the world you have to do other than to practice that one technique which may take less than a minute to do. It may take twice as long to quiet down as to do the exercise. But for that short time, there is no tomorrow.

The performer doesn't do the essential exercise but worries about not getting on with scene study. Everyone wants to be where the action is. And it's hard for anyone to convince us that the real action is somewhere else.

Why is it so hard to practice?

It takes a long time to calm down to start the exercises, and then nothing much happens in your first efforts. You can get away with not doing them and still function. You can even perform and get praise.

Exercises are not ego gratifying. They are boring. You are isolated, lifting a leg ten times or releasing the jaw hinge, while the whole world is partying.

≈≈≈

If you feel any eagerness when you start to work, if the body tightens anywhere, you are not ready. You have to disengage from the exercise more and still more until you have taught yourself not to be eager, not to want it – for the wrong reasons. By now you know what those are.

It takes as much discipline to not do as to do.

Putting ego and despair and all that to the side for the moment, using simple objective discipline and doing your exercise because you say you will, will get you through. No peripheral desire. You get to like practicing at some point and don't find it tedious. Process becomes interesting and enlightening. You begin to feel subtle physical sensations that were not available to you previously. You begin to trust your exercises; they give you stability and, if you can believe this, eventually you do them with affection. They are dependable, like friends, close and supportive.

This is the bottom line, folks.

ACKNOWLEDGEMENTS

I get by with the help of my friends:

I could not have written the book as logically as I was able to without the close reading that Mary Waldorf gave to each chapter, each paragraph of each chapter while I was writing it. I thank her for those single-spaced, four-page critiques she sent me. Although I despaired upon getting them, I wrote a better chapter after absorbing her comments.

My thanks to my singing teacher, Alice Rowe, the guardian of my released jaw hinge, my deliciously fat tongue, and my breath moving to my words, who corrected me when I tried too hard. Over and above that of giving information, Alice Rowe's was the most unselfish teaching I have ever encountered.

Mark and Josephine Harris have always been supportive and incredibly generous taking time to read my work and giving me their seasoned comments.

I've had very caring students. They were part of my growth as I was of theirs. It was Tian Dayton who plopped one of those marbleized boxes down in front of me and said "You are going to write your acting book. Fill this with notes." Fill it I did until it was so full it broke at the seams. Then I knew I had to face the organization of all those notes.

Ruth Cox supported me with a quiet strength from the first to the last day of writing.

A group of artists, talking one night, agreed that every one needs a mentor — someone old enough to be supportive, to give that extra push. I was lucky. The great character actress Aline MacMahon did that for me.

I am grateful to Judy Leibowitz for my Alexander Technique lessons and to Janice Seaman who gave me a glimpse into the mystery of Tai Chi and Yoga.

And for explanations from their disciplines, my thanks to Janet Lewis Winters, Professor Ruby Cohn, Dr. Deborah Wesley, and Professor Leonid Hambro.

Professor Len Pronko, a foremost theater historian and a master of the art of Kabuki, read the manuscript and recommended it to Glenn Young, Mr. Applause Books himself. I am grateful for that and for the pleasure of his company.

My children, Tara and Jonathan, are always there for me. I seem to give my best performance when my son Dick Blau is in the audience.

My thanks to Gordon Lyle Pollack, the artist, who did the diagrams.

INDEX

MONOLOGUE WORKSHOP

From Search to Discovery
in Audition and Performance

by Jack Poggi

To those for whom the monologue has always been synonymous with terror, *The Monologue Workshop* will prove an indispensable ally. Jack Poggi's new book answers the long-felt need among actors for top-notch guidance in finding, rehearsing and performing monologues. For those who find themselves groping for speech just hours before their "big break," this book is their guide to salvation.

The Monologue Workshop supplies the tools to discover new pieces before they become over-familiar, excavate older material that has been neglected, and adapt material from non-dramatic sources (novels, short stories, letters, diaries, autobiographies, even newspaper columns). There are also chapters on writing original monologues and creating solo performances in the style of Lily Tomlin and Eric Bogosian.

Besides the wealth of practical advice he offers, Poggi transforms the monologue experience from a terrifying ordeal into an exhilarating opportunity. Jack Poggi, as many working actors will attest, is the actor's partner in a process they had always thought was without one.

paper•ISBN 1-55783-031-2 • $12.95

ON SINGING ONSTAGE

New, Completely Revised Edition

by David Craig

"David Craig KNOWS MORE ABOUT SINGING IN THE MUSICAL THEATRE THAN ANYONE IN THIS COUNTRY ... SHORT OF TAKING CLASSES, THIS BOOK IS A MUST."   —Harold Prince

"David Craig, through his training has miraculously fused the art of acting and singing. HE HAS PUT THE WINGS OF TALENT ON HIS STUDENTS."   —Stella Adler

PAPER • ISBN: 1-55783-043-6

A PERFORMER PREPARES

A Guide to Song Preparation for Actors, Singers, and Dancers

by David Craig

A Performer Prepares is a class act magically transformed to the printed page. It's a thirteen-part master-class on how to perform, on any stage from bleak rehearsal room to the Palace Theater. The class will cover the basic Broadway song numbers, from Show Ballad to Showstopper. With precise, logical steps and dynamic and entertaining dialogues between himself and his students, Craig takes anyone with the desire to shine from an audition to final curtain call, recreating the magic of his New York and L.A. coaching sessions.

CLOTH • ISBN: 1-55783-133-5

SPEAK WITH DISTINCTION
by Edith Skinner

"Speak With Distinction is the **most comprehensive and accessible speech book available** for teachers and students of speech."
— Joan Washington, RSC, Royal Court
& Royal National Theatre

"Edith Skinner's book is the **best book on speech I have ever encountered**. It was my primer in school and it is my reference book now. To the classical actor, or for that matter any actor who wishes to be understood, this method is a sure guide."
— Kevin Kline

"Speak with Distinction is **the single most important work on the actor's craft** of stage speech. Edith Skinner's work must be an indispensable source book for all who aspire to act."
— Earle Gister, Yale School of Drama

paper•ISBN 1–155783–047–9

APPLAUSE